For : le

īs

Eddie!

Face to Face

Interviews Across
Time and Space

Volume 1: The Classic Series

Eddie McGuigan

Obverse Books
info@obversebooks.co.uk
www.obversebooks.co.uk
Cover Design by Cody Quijano-Schell
First published November 2013

I'd like to dedicate this book to the people who made it possible for me to talk to the heroes of my childhood, something I've never, ever taken for granted.

As well as all the interviewees who took time to speak to me, I'd like to single out Mark Strickson, Frazer Hines, Philip Hinchcliffe, Tom Baker, Colin Baker, Katy Manning, Louise Jameson, John Leeson and Daphne Ashbrook for continuing support.

Nicholas Briggs, Paul Spragg and everyone at Big Finish, for believing, standing by and great advice

And of course the boys of Outpost Skaro, without whom I would have had none of these interviews:
Derek Dunnington, Alan Reilly, Nic Ford, Kyle Barghout, Andy Zahl, Tony Ingram and David Hookham.

Special mention for help on a couple of the interviews for David Adams and Jeremy Richardson

As always, Lee Mansfield.

And finally, my editor, Stuart Douglas, for going "f*%k it, let's do it!" Wonderful chaps, all of them!

Contents

Foreword

Hello there, Faithful Reader!

First of all let me thank you for buying this book, renting it from the library or borrowing it from a friend! Even if you only got it for £1 in the bargain bucket, thank you for having the interest in it and wanting to have a look inside.

What lies beyond is a chronological voyage through the history of your (and my) favourite television show – and, as we both know, faithful reader, the best television show in the world! – *Doctor Who*!

I hope you enjoy reading the conversations which follow as much as I enjoyed having them. It never stops being a thrill when I speak to a personal hero, and make no mistake; every single person I've spoken to in this book is a bona fide hero of mine. They helped shape my childhood, my attitudes and my route through life, and speaking to them face to face was a thrill beyond description.

A little housekeeping before you open that creaky blue door – some of these interviews were first published on the website *Outpost Skaro* (but are no longer available there due to a regeneration on that site), and as such as are time specific – or chronologically inhibited as K9 might say (chapter four, John Leeson...). As such, I discuss with those interviewees specific things which were pertinent at the time, so you may read about a book that's already released, or an audio you've already bought (and if not, why not!?).

Not all the interviews have been published before though – many are unique to this publication and it's been my privilege to collect them and speak to the people involved.

For me as a fan, it's given me a fascinating insight into not just how this wonderful, wonderful programme is made, but the people who make it; all of whom, bar none, have been friendly, courteous, professional and enthusiastic. They, too, are fans.

The twelfth Doctor, Peter Capaldi, said it perfectly when he said "Doctor Who belongs to us all!"

Who am I to argue with the Doctor? As the programme does, so does this book.

Happy times and places

Eddie

The First Doctor Era
"Eh? Doctor who? What's he talking about...?"

The First Doctor's tenure was a masterclass in catching lightning in a bottle. But it really shouldn't have worked.

Original creator, Sydney Newman, hated the theme tune, the lead actor and the Daleks. CE Webber, one of the creative forces behind the characterisations of the main characters, was described by Newman as "nuts" for some of his suggestions. Producer Verity Lambert was a young woman, poached from ITV and given the job of presenting this unique, crazy series with no experience and very little backing from the BBC Sixth Floor, who saw an eleven week run of space adventures to fill a gap. Director Waris Hussein thought he was better than children's television and hated the idea of the first adventure, 'An Unearthly Child', being set mainly in the stone age, with characters who couldn't talk. Even designer Peter Brachacki was dismissive of the job, despite producing an ultra modern iconic masterpiece.

Nothing should have worked, and yet it did - and then some. But why?

In the first instance credit has to go to the Doctor. Ironically, the first thing the Doctor ever saved was himself, and in the form of William Hartnell the programme found its biggest fan.

Tired of playing angry and hard, Hartnell seized on the character of the Doctor and made him the man he would be for the next fifty years. He was clever, dark, irascible and fun. But more than anything, Hartnell took the role seriously. With immense passion and huge conviction, the Doctor came to life and evolved over the first two series. Along with companions Barbara and Ian (Jacqueline Hill and William Russell) and granddaughter Susan (Carole Ann Ford), Hartnell created something new for this fledging adventure series.

Carole Ann Ford

Recently, the role of *Who* girl has been one which has been much sought after by young actors, and a frequently discussed topic in the popular media. It has helped springboard (or restart) careers and attracted performers as diverse as Catherine Tate and Billie Piper, but it was Carole Ann Ford – elfin, beautiful and alien – who created the template everyone else has followed, and it is against her that every subsequent companion should be measured.

As part of the original TARDIS crew she was responsible for helping shape the programme we know today, and her role in this cannot be over-estimated. I spoke to her about Susan Foreman – the Doctor's granddaughter, let's not forget – in the wake of her reappearance in the Big Finish audio adventure, 'An Earthly Child'.

I wondered first what had made Carole want to become an actress?

"I always wanted to be 'on the stage', so I started as a dancer at eleven, but got pneumonia, so couldn't do that anymore. School plays and amateur led to professional acting. The role in 'Man On A Bicycle' led to me getting *Doctor Who*…"

Susan Foreman was one of a kind – the first Who girl. But she was more than that. She was a fellow Time Lord, a refugee just like the Doctor, and also, as will be explored soon in "An Earthly Child", the Doctor's Granddaughter! Did you develop the character herself or was it given to you?

"She came from Gallifrey, when her grandfather had to get away because of an argument/difference of opinion with the Time Lords. Bill (William Hartnell) and I made the backstory up together."

Famously, the first episode was reshot at the bequest of the Powers that Be. I wondered if Carole had approached Susan differently second time around?

"Yes, I originally wanted to make her to be weirder, more interesting."

I asked Carole about the fan train of thought that Susan isn't exactly the Doctor's granddaughter, but more a contemporary of him, or something else? How does she feel about that?

"That's not what we were told, that's all speculation. I don't know where that came from."

The rest of the original TARDIS crew were older and more established than Carole had been, and it seems that Billy took the grandfather role rather literally when it came to the younger actress… how was it to walk into that type of dynamic?

"Terrifying! But we all got on very well, very quickly. Bill tried to be controlling and I resisted, but he meant well and only wanted the best for me."

It seems the old legend of him being difficult to work with is all a matter of opinion – his companions didn't always think so.

"He was a darling. He had a great sense of humour, quite naughty sometimes, but a perfectionist with strong opinions that he didn't mind voicing."

I wondered if Carole felt anything special in that TARDIS set, originally. Did she sense something special was happening?

"No, but, obviously, it was something very different. Breaking previous boundaries. But, ultimately, it was just another job."

And another first, the journey into space and time, for the first time, landed the intrepid new friends on Skaro, and the most iconic episode of Doctor Who of all time – 'The Daleks"! I asked Carole how they were to work with, and if she got a sense of history in the making with them?

"We thought that they were very funny! Although interesting and innovative. But we'd no idea they would have such an impact."

Following from that, 'The Edge of Destruction' is a wonderful piece of enclosed Who, allowing each of the characters the flex their acting muscles. Was Carole happy with the scripts in general?

"'The Edge of Destruction' was my favourite story to act in. Scripts varied, some brilliant, some not so good, but mostly frustrating for me, as they were rather repetitive."

And did she have a favourite between the historical and science fiction ones?

"Historical. I preferred Historical ones."

And in 'The Dalek Invasion of Earth' we say farewell to Susan... how did this happen?

"It was my choice to leave. My character was getting rather boring, she was never really developed. I don't think they knew what to do with me."

13

And how did the rest of the cast take the news?

"Oh they weren't very happy. Especially Bill."

And the exit itself? A lot of commentators have suggested it's a little abrupt...?

"I would rather have gone on a more upbeat note rather than for 'true love'. I would have liked Susan's abilities to have been recognised more and to have been used in the recreation of the world."

I pointed out that this indeed was the case in some of the spin off material, in the "what happened next" category.

"Oh, I wasn't aware of that, no."

Carole has always been happy to be associated with Doctor Who, *and it has of course endured. What's its secret?*

"It made such an impact on the public, there was nothing else out there like it and it appealed to all ages and all types of people."

And she returned to Doctor Who *twenty years later for 'The Five Doctors'. Of course, sadly Billy had passed on since then, and the First Doctor was played by the rather unFirst Doctorish Richard Hurndall... was that weird?*

"It was very strange. Richard Hurndall was great in the part and we also had a good relationship. But it was strange."

I thought that maybe, considering who Susan is, something more could have been made with her interacting with the other incarnations?

"That's an interesting thought!"

And now, of course, she gets the chance to do just that when she meets the Doctor again – now in his eighth life in "An Earthly Child". What's that adventure like? Carole is tight lipped but will say: "Only that it is a totally fascinating and exciting twist. The fans must discover the rest by listening to it. I don't want to spoil it for them."

But working with Paul [McGann] must have been an experience. A very different Doctor to Bill...

"Totally different. Much younger, of course, but as soon as we started working together than same old indefinable magic happened. It helped that Paul is a very good and exciting actor."

And a lovely twist in the dynamic of the Doctor and Susan...

"You'll just have to listen to it!"

I turned to the new series – I presume she's aware of it and watches it?

"I've been loving the new series, but the Doctors are getting younger and younger!"

And younger again. Others suggested on his casting that Matt [Smith] might be a little too young. Does Carole think so?

"I agree in theory, but let's wait and see. Although we might end up with a twelve year old at this rate!"

And the new series isn't a stranger to bringing back old companions. Would Carole go back?

"I would love to! But I think it would be an almost impossible task for the script writers, though I have a few ideas if they are interested. And the fans keep sending me ideas too!"

And a final spoiler... go on... what've you got coming up in the future?

"More stories on CD with Big Finish."

I'm glad, after fifty years, Susan Foreman is still out there, fighting the good fight.

Peter Purves

It is curious that there is this myth surrounding William Hartnell being difficult to work with. It doesn't really seem to be the case for the actors who knew him. What comes through more than anything is his passion for the programme and his love of the character.

As the series evolved, though, Carole Ann was joined in departure by William Russell and Jacqueline Hill, and a new leading man was required. Step forward Peter Purves, who played Steven Taylor, space pilot, and who discussed with me not just *Doctor Who*, but his iconic roles on TV over the last forty-five years.

Purves is a British institution, not only for his ten *Doctor Who* stories in the mid 60s, but for his eleven years on the seminal children's magazine programme *Blue Peter* and his twelve years on another iconic programme, *Kick Start*. Add to that a memorable appearance on Ricky Gervais' *The Office* and his ever present safe-hands influence on *Crufts*, Peter Purves is a living British TV Legend.

When I spoke to him, he was amiable, enthusiastic and had a wonderful recall of his time on *Doctor Who* – as well as his time on his other landmark shows.

Did going to school in Blackpool affect what you wanted to be as an adult? Was acting always the thing for you?

"Yes. Blackpool was the Mecca for show business at that time, particularly in the summer. So I saw a lot of shows as a child, and wanted to be an actor from the age of nine."

You'd done a few "one off" roles before Doctor Who – Dixon of Dock Green, Armchair Thriller, The Villains… do any of them stand out to you?

"*Armchair Theatre* stood out – it was my first leading role on TV and as it was a character who was a beach photographer from Blackpool, it was the perfect role for me[iii]. I also enjoyed my leading role in *The Villains[iv]*, with a good friend of mine, the actor Mike Pratt (Randall and Hopkirk deceased)."

And then came a guest role in 'The Chase'… do you know you share a commonality with actors Lalla Ward, Freema Agyeman and Karen Gillan as you appeared in the series as someone else but became a companion soon after? How did this come about?

"The director Richard Martin turned me down for a role as a giant insect in an earlier episode of *Doctor Who* ('The Web Planet'), but promised me a decent acting role if one should come about. It did, he was as good as his word, and I played Morton Dill for him in 'The Chase', episode three.

"It was a successful performance for me, because after the recording, Verity Lambert, the producer, and Dennis Spooner, [story editor] invited me for a drink and offered me the part of Steven Taylor. I have the distinction of playing two different characters in the same serial, because Steven's first appearance was in episode six of 'The Chase'."

How did you approach Steven Taylor? On paper he is, of course, the replacement for Ian Chesterton, but you brought a lot more to him than that…

"I am an instinctive actor, and I just played the character as he came off the page. I liked the idea of Steven, but was disappointed with some of the scripts that didn't really give the character enough scope or range.

Actually there was only one that I really hated and that was my second serial, 'Galaxy 4'"

Why was that?

"'Galaxy Four' was a strange story - quite good in its way, but the writer [William Emms - Ed] had not been told that I had replaced Jackie and Russ in the series. Consequently, the storyline, which had featured Jackie, had been adapted for me to take that role - only it meant Steven was incredibly weak, having been captured by the four Drahvin women. Actually it could have been an imprisonment to die for, but it didn't really make any sense. There were some serious problems, technically, in the studio, so after the euphoria of my first serial ['The Time Meddler'] 'Galaxy 4' was a considerable disappointment."

Which were worse to work with, Daleks or Mechanoids?

"Both were terrible!"

Your first "full" story is 'The Meddling Monk' – another seminal Doctor Who *episode, in that it's the first to feature another Time Lord. Where you aware at the time it was something special? What are your memories of it?*

"I liked the serial and enjoyed working with Bill, Maureen and, of course, the superb and lovely Peter Butterworth[v]. My memories of it are that it was a good job to have got! I had a good time with the character and with the cast!"

How important do you think the role of the companion is? Do you think it's different now from when you did it?

"The whole show has changed in concept, and although I think the new stuff is very good, I think it misses some of the original thinking. I liked the serendipity of the TARDIS being uncontrollable (i.e. broken) so the Doctor never knew where he was going to end up."

You know, looking at your ten adventures with the Doctor, it strikes me as to how many iconic ones there are; it was a really rich seam being struck. What are your memories of stories like 'The Celestial Toymaker' and 'The Gunfighters'?

"'The Celestial Toymaker' was a favourite right from the start, and Michael Gough[vi] was an interesting actor with whom to work. Carmen Silvera[vii] was a joy, and the storyline was really very clever. As to 'The Gunfighters', I didn't really like it at the time, but I have seen it since, and it is quite a good funny script, and the performances aren't bad at all. I think it was not much fun to work on because the director, Rex Tucker didn't give any time to directing me and Jackie Lane. We were the regulars in the cast, and as he didn't cast us he didn't pay us much heed or attention."

Did you know of the suggestion that William Hartnell was originally to be leaving during 'The Celestial Toymaker'? (apparently the Toymaker would have 're-arranged' what the Doctor looked like).

"The serial was the second attempt to see if the show worked without the Doctor - they were trying to find a way to write Bill out, but it didn't happen straight away as you know. Bill took three weeks holiday and only appeared as a disembodied hand after the first episode."

I know that William Hartnell was becoming ill by the time you joined, and I know you must have been asked a million times how difficult he was, but, researching that time, it seems to me you struck a bit of a rapport with him and that, despite his crotchetiness, you were able to relate with him. How was he?

"I enjoyed Bill's company, he was kind and generous to me, and we struck up some sort of friendship. He often took me for lunch, and seemed to try to mentor me (I was a very inexperienced TV actor at the time). I watched him persecute some directors, and also have no rapport with a lot of the guesting actors, but with me, Maureen and Jackie, he could be delightful."

In 'The Dalek Masterplan' the role of the companion became somewhat tenuous with both Katarina and Sara Kingdom dying during the episode. What were your thoughts on that? Not usual fare for a children's series…

"Total surprise when Katarina died. I thought she was supposed to have been the new permanent companion replacing the beautiful Maureen O'Brien. Jean Marsh, on the other hand knew she was only going to survive to the end of the serial. It was a good story line in that respect. She was never really the Doctor's travelling companion, just a character who joined us for a while."

You left with 'The Savages'… was this your choice? What was your thinking behind leaving?

"It wasn't my choice – Innes Lloyd, the producer, decided arbitrarily that companions would only stay for one year at a time. I wasn't happy about being written out, and Bill was furious, little knowing that his days on the show were numbered too."

After Doctor Who *you continued to act – noticeably returning to* Z Cars[viii] *for instance, and then* Blue Peter[ix] *came along… how did that happen?*

"Pure fluke really. Two dinner parties that I knew nothing of resulted in my name being given to the *Blue Peter* producers who then contacted my agent (actually my ex-agent because they had just said I would have to get some different representation as they couldn't get me any work!). I then contacted the BBC and was invited to meet Biddy Baxter and her team, and then auditioned a couple of times before being offered the 'best job in TV'."

Blue Peter *seemed to put on hold your acting career. Was that frustrating? Or were you happy to move into presenting?*

"After I learned how to do it, I enjoyed being a presenter. But it was a hard job learning how 'not to act'."

You struck up a wonderful rapport with your co-presenters on Blue Peter... *what a lot of people consider the "definitive" line-up is yourself, John Noakes, Valerie Singleton and later Lesley Judd. Did you all get on in "real life" as you seem to onscreen?*

"Yes, and we remain good friends to this day."

The expeditions look both exhilarating and perhaps a lot of hard work...do any stand out to you? What was your favourite/worst?

"All of the expeditions were a joy – one of the favourites was the expedition to Morocco. I think it is because we had such a varied time – the stories were fun to work on, and I think Marrakesh is the most foreign place I have ever visited. Quite wonderful and exciting. The worst was probably Brunei. It was a dull country in many ways. The only reason for its existence is the oil, which meant there were many expats working there. The film with the former head-hunters in their Long Huts was pretty interesting, and the short film on jungle survival was fun, but on the whole it wasn't the best trip I've been on."

What do you think the enduring appeal of Blue Peter *is?*

"I have no idea other than the fact that its values have always been good, its production team has been excellent, and there is always a new audience growing into and out of the show."

And I suppose, I should ask the same question about Doctor Who?

"That is a bigger imponderable. I have no idea why the show has continued so long, or become such a cult show. It has changed a lot since its inception, yet somehow it has captured the imagination of an ever-growing audience"

And during that time you managed to do an awful lot of Doctor Who *promotions – even having Jon Pertwee bring in the Whomobile! You knew Jon personally, didn't you? How did you find him?*

"I liked Jon a lot. I never really liked him as the Doctor, but he was a splendid man. My wife and I had many a dinner with him and his wife, Ingeborg, both in the UK and on the island of Ibiza. He became a good friend. The last time I saw him was at a convention in Manchester – he had just had some surgery for skin cancer, apart from which he seemed very well."

You left Blue Peter *in 1978… was that a personal choice? Why did you leave?*

"That was my choice. I came home from a holiday in Greece and just thought it was time move on. The producers agreed, and asked me to stay a further six months up until Easter 1978. I did, and the BBC kindly offered me a number of series' to work on – *Stopwatch*, *We're Going Places*, and *Blue Peter Specials*. Other shows came along, and the eighties were a very busy and successful time for me."

And then on to Kick Start for, what, twelve years? What are your memories of that?

"I was so disappointed when *Kickstart* and *Junior Kickstart*[x] ended. The promoter, Nick Brittain, couldn't get the sponsorship necessary to make the shows. The sponsors changed twice – Norwich Union and Lombard Tricity supported the programme for most of the time, and it was a great show to work on. But it only took a weekend to make the entire series. "

You've played 'a presenter' a few times – maybe due to your own corporate films career – and of course famously appeared in The Office[xi]. *How did that come about? Did you get to work directly with Gervais and Merchant?*

"I was asked by Ricky to appear on his Channel 4 chat show from the Trafalgar Studios, and after the show he told me he was planning a series that the BBC had commissioned. I suggested that if he ever needed an old fart like me then give me a call. He did, and I made the corporate video insert for *The Office*. Great fun, played dead straight, (apart from the last line). I have been asked many times if I objected to one of my old corporate videos being used on the show. It wasn't old. It was made especially for *The Office!*"

You're well known for your amiable and enthusiastic willingness to be associated with Doctor Who, *even after this time. How have fans been with you?*

"Very supportive usually – because I haven't attended a lot of *Doctor Who* events, I think I am still a bit of a novelty."

Have you seen any of the new series? If so what do you think of it, and the Doctor now?

"I am not a regular viewer, but what I have seen looks extremely professional to me. It is shot like a film – when I was in the show it was done as a continuous 'as live' recording – and has all the benefits of modern technology going for it. I like David Tennant and thought he was a good choice. I also liked Christopher Eccleston. But I am not sure about this new twenty something. I'll give him a chance, but it doesn't fit the image I would expect."

There has of course been a couple of successful old companions return – Sarah Jane and K9 – and now there are rumours that a sixties' companion is to appear in the new series… could you envisage Steven Taylor reappearing with the Doctor? It would be a nice role reversal, perhaps, and a story to tell…?

"I would jump at the chance".

Anneke Wills

As Peter said, the new production crew on *Doctor Who* may have been looking to replace the increasingly ill and temperamental William Hartnell as early as 'The Celestial Toymaker', but they had a problem – how do you replace the titular character from one of the most popular programmes on television?

As Hartnell became more unwell, new script editor Gerry Davis and producer Innes Lloyd came up with what is probably the most important idea in the show's history. Whilst not actually called this until 1973, the concept of *regenerating* the Doctor suddenly made the programme immortal.

So, as the first Doctor barely escaped his first battle with the Cybermen on 29th October 1966, he collapsed on the TARDIS floor and something miraculous happened – Patrick Troughton appeared.

I asked one of the companions who saw that transition, Anneke Wills, about her time on the series…

How did you get the role in Doctor Who*?*

"Usual route – agent sends me for an interview at the BBC!"

How was Bill to work with? I've heard he could be difficult, but both Carole Ann and Peter say he was great, if you knew how to work him.

"I think Peter and Carole Ann had the best of him — by the time Mike and I joined he was getting very tired, ill and crotchety. We joined not knowing that his time was coming to an end."

What was the mood like when he was leaving?

"Very poignant."

How different, professionally, was Pat from Bill? Frazer tells me of great times of laughs and pranks.

"Perhaps because Bill was such hard work, Patrick seemed like heaven to work with. So creative and funny, humble, sweet, brilliant — everything we missed working with Bill."

Were you satisfied with the role of Polly?

"At the time, yes, I was just happy to have work."

Did you see Ben as integral to Polly? Would they have worked separately?

"Perhaps because we were such supportive friends at once (we were committed mates during the difficulties with Billy), when they told him to leave, I left too. We were a team."

Was that your only reason for leaving?

"No, there were a few reasons — to support Mike, because I thought it was bit mean the way they axed him. I also didn't want to be typecast and also because my darling little children hadn't seen much of their mum for a year."

Would you resurrect Polly for the TV again?

"Well she has been resurrected already for Big Finish, so I'm very satisfied with those stories."

We then spoke about her stories individually...

"'The War Machines' – the start of it all. We were very excited to join the *Doctor Who* team.

'The Smugglers' – Loved the story and the location in Cornwall. And the costumes!

'The Tenth Planet' – tricky times with Bill leaving, and being about! David Dodimead[xii] had a wonderful sense of humour, which was definitely needed! And it was our first meeting with the Cybermen!

'Power of the Daleks' – such fun beginning to work with Patrick and our first (well Ben and Polly's!) encounter with the Daleks

'The Highlanders' – a great story! Mike and I loved this one! Patrick is very funny in it.

'The Underwater Menace' – Pat was very worried about this story not being good enough. I hated my uncomfortable shell costume.

'The Moonbase' – We all loved this story. Pat Barr[xiii] is a great actor – but the Gravitron nearly killed the Doctor!

'The Macra Terror' – oh we had to work hard on this one to make it seem real. The crabs were a bit clunky.

'The Faceless Ones' – Ah. Sad times. It was a sad one. Because we were departing and knowing how much we would miss being in *Doctor Who*."

The Second Doctor Era

Renewed? Have I? That's it, I've been renewed. It's part of the TARDIS. Without it I couldn't survive.

Let's not underestimate Patrick Troughton's importance in the canon of *Doctor Who*.

Without him there would be no modern *Doctor Who* at all. Whilst William Hartnell helped make the show a phenomenon, Patrick Troughton honed the style which to this day endures, and created traits which all Doctors – especially Matt Smith – have used in their own versions of the character.

With Patrick no longer with us, I asked his son, actor Michael Troughton, about his dad's time as the iconic Time Lord...

Michael Troughton

Patrick taking over the lead was a massive gamble for both him and the series, as it hadn't been done before. Was he aware of this?

"The pressure on my father to come up with a new Doctor must have been extremely high. One newspaper clipping my mother has kept reported,

'William Hartnell as Doctor Who was very human and warmly appealing. With him lay the series peculiar character. The new Doctor Who is Patrick Troughton and with the change the very substance of the series lies in the melting pot. [xiv]

It is clear his worries were also centred round the undeniable fear he felt of being typecast. He had worked very hard during the 1950's and early sixties to establish himself as a highly respected and successful TV character actor. He felt that accepting a role like Doctor Who would almost definitely destroy this reputation and everything he had set out to do. He revelled in the freedom of being able to create such individual and different characterisations each time he was offered a TV role. This could all be taken away from him as the public and profession labelled him Doctor Who Two."

It's well publicised that he was keen to be in complete disguise as the Doctor but this was vetoed. Was he happy with the "cosmic hobo" persona he took on?
"Pat found the process of creating character ideas contradictory and frustrating. A number of wildly varying characterisations formed from personal rehearsal sessions at home including appearing as the Victorian Prime Minister Gladstone complete with mutton-chop side burns, a mad

scientist with spiky black hair and a ridiculously high voice, and a turban headed character out of the *Arabian Nights*. He showed me a number of sketches completed in a black A4 sized notebook with annotated scribbles. One was a picture of a Mississippi paddle steamer captain who wore a dark uniform and naval cap. I think it was supposed to look like a character that W. C. Fields[xv] had once played in a movie. Another was a pirate with an eye-patch similar to the part he had played in the Disney film version of *Treasure Island*. On the last page was a tramp with tattered clothes and a tall felt hat, pushing an old pram full of his belongings and playing an old tin whistle. I remember David asking him why so many of his ideas involved such elaborate disguises to which he replied, 'I don't want anyone to know who is playing Who! I think it took him a good three or four stories to become happy with his tramp like character."

As a character actor of immense quality, how close to Patrick Troughton was the Doctor in personality?

"Certain elements of the character were a little like him but he was a professional actor who drew both on his own experience and what he saw in the world around him. He would have said – it's all pretend. The actor and the character are two separate things."

Frazer [Hines] tells of pranks and laughs during their tenure. Was he happy in the role?
"Yes – he told me they were the happiest years in his professional life."

Why did he decide to leave?

"As Dad later explained in an interview,

'You could stay with it, and they wanted me to, for as long as the BBC did it or they got tired of you. That might be at best, one thought, five years. That would have been eight years, and by then one would have been so connected with the character that getting other work would have been very difficult indeed. So that was the main consideration there. Or one could leave. Give up a fortune. And that's what we decided to do'[xvi]."

Was he happy with the way Who *stuck to him through his life? He always seemed keen to come back (in the Three, Five and Two Doctors...)*

"Dad was always keen to play the doctor. But I do remember having this conversation with him the first time he was asked to reprise the part. 'Do I really want the public to see me as the Doctor again after all the hard work I have done to make them forget?'

I told him he should find out what the fee was before he dismissed it! He laughed and retorted, 'I've taught you well!'"

Did he regret leaving when he did?
"No. He had done enough and he was still worried about type casting."

You were, what, ten, when he became the Doctor? Was it a big deal for you? I imagine it's like your Dad being Superman.

"Wonderful feeling at the time. I was twelve. Best thing was going to school the day after it had hit the news."

What do you think he would think of the new series and the fact it's reached fifty?

"He would be amazed it has lasted as long as it has. After all when he took the part he thought it would only go on for six weeks."

How would you like to see him remembered for the celebrations?

"I have already celebrated his memory at the BFI event in February. Everyone there told me he was the most respected of all the Doctors because if it hadn't been for his strong performance the series would never have reached the fiftieth year. I certainly agree with them but I'm biased!"

Frazer Hines

We've spoken a lot about Frazer Hines. As the iconic Jamie McCrimmon, he has been an ambassador for *Doctor Who* since his first appearance, and continues to be to this day.

Spending an hour in the company of a bona fide *Doctor Who* legend is another treat. Frazer Hines is that incarnate. A mighty figure from a Golden Age of *Doctor Who*, he embodies all that was genius about the Troughton Years. The enthusiasm, the grace, the friendliness and the sheer joy the man has for the series is infectious. It echoes the approach the maestro Patrick Troughton had and resonates through to today. For me, as much as the second Doctor, he *is* the Troughton Years. Not only does he have great memories of the time, he channels the Doctor himself – speaking in staccato from Frazer, to Jamie, to the Doctor. It really is a thing to behold.

Interrupted only by a moo-ing kettle – for a second, I thought we were on *Emmerdale Farm* – I turned on the Mind Probe and spoke to Frazer – and the Second Doctor – on the progression of a young Jacobite boy from rebel to *Who* Colossus.

He'd begun his professional career as a child, and I asked how that had happened.

"I used to go to a song and dance school when we lived in Harrogate in North Yorkshire, and I quite enjoyed it and did this impression of

Maurice Chevalier[xvii] and someone saw me from the Corona School[xviii] and I joined there down in London."

Frazer was quite successful as a child actor, and I wondered how hard this was to maintain.

"I started off in crowd screens in movies, so it was quite hard, because television was in its infancy."

Was the role as Jamie anything to do with his role in The Young Jacobites[xix]?

"No, it was a coincidence really, I'd played a lot of Scots boys in plays, different plays, then in *The Young Jacobites* with Jeremy Bullock who went on to play - was it Jabba the Hutt?"

Boba Fett.

"Yeah, that's it! Boba Fett. But I got the part of Jamie because I'd worked with Shaun Sutton[xx]."

I pointed out that Jamie was one of the longest running companions – was he aware of that?

"Yes, I knew that – in fact, I found out recently that Jamie was the fourth most popular companion and the rest were all from the new series, like Sarah Jane and Catherine Tate...

"He's a character I loved playing. And I loved returning to him too with Colin Baker in Big Finish... stepping into the recording booth all the years just swept away."

Was it easy returning?

"Yes, so easy!"

I asked Frazer about his time with Patrick, who he worked with in all but one of his stories.

"Oh, what a wonderful man. So giving and forgiving. A lovely man, a great man to work with. Great fun."

I was astounded by his impression of Patrick in the audios.

"I like to listen to those on a long car journey. It came about by accident, telling an anecdote in a convention where I 'did' Patrick in a story. About four years ago I did it in my first Big Finish audio and the producer/director asked if I could keep it up, and asked why I didn't just do the voice, so I did, and every time I do a Big Finish or BBC I always ask if they want it.

"I don't work on it, I always like doing impressions, so it comes naturally. When I do the performance, I feel when I step into the booth Patrick comes in too, because I do the hand movements too. It's great to do."

I told Frazer that some fans been discussing whether Big Finish should recast the first three Doctors in the audios, and that we'd all come to the conclusion that it would have to be something very special – or someone very special like himself or David Troughton – to be accepted in that role. Would Frazer every play the Second Doctor?

"I haven't heard David. Has he done it?"

I don't think he has.

"I would though, absolutely. Although they say that David has Patrick's cough – and it's something I do too, but I do that naturally, because it's something he did without thinking."

I watched 'The War Games' and 'The Three Doctors' recently, and it struck me how modern Patrick's Doctor was – he'd fit in today, wouldn't he?

"Yeah, fit in, and happily wreck the new TARDIS as well."

You must have learned a lot from a maestro like him?

"Oh yes. We adlibbed a lot, added things in. Like Jamie telling him he should press this or that button, and the Doctor grumpily smacking his hand away, we added that. Some directors like Michael Ferguson or Dougie Camfield would happily allow us to do that, but others were a bit more strict with the script – if it wasn't written we couldn't do it. It was a lovely thing when we were allowed too."

Obviously Frazer, Wendy and Pat all left at once – was that deliberate?

"Well, I'd done three years and my agent at the time said "right, darling, it's time to move on, do some films etc" and I'd said "no, I want to stay…" but she wanted me to leave, so Patrick said, "Well, hang on, my contract expires in six months, why don't you wait…" cos he was getting earache from his wife saying "why are you still there? You should be doing other stuff rather than a children's serial…" because, to be honest, in 1967 it was a kids' Saturday evening serial, so they made us leave. I often say that if they hadn't then Patrick and I would still be there now, you'd've had to shoot us to get us away and out of the TARDIS. We had so much fun. I'd've liked to have worked with Pertwee, see how it went, but I wonder if we would have captured that same sense of fun."

Considering the changes in glamorous leading ladies – and Michael Craze of course – did that sense of fun, that dynamic, change during his time in the role?

"I don't think so – Anneke and Michael were the team when I joined and I was this interloper. We're great friends now, of course, but at the time I felt it was "there's three of us in the TARDIS, we don't need three," and I was the spare part."

The original concept, of course, was to have three in the TARDIS.

"That's true, but, of course, when Patrick and I had decided to leave, Wendy said, "well, you're not leaving me with Pertwee because he's so tall and I'm so small… we'd never get a close up!" So she left too."

Soon after Doctor Who Frazer got another icon role in that of Joe Sugden on Emmerdale Farm. *How did that happen?*

"I used to go out with an actress called Lisa Goddard, and we remained friends for ages and I had lunch with her at her house one day and her father, David Goddard, who I'd worked with at the BBC as a little boy before he went to Australia and produced *Skippy*, and I asked what he was doing now, and he was casting this Yorkshire soap – they had the mother and the eldest son, but the didn't have the youngest son – so Lisa said "Daddy, Frazer is from Yorkshire, and if you don't cast him, mummy and I are leaving home!" So I got the part!"

And you were there for – what was it? Twelve years?

"Eleven years. I left because I got married, then went back and did another six years."

Is Frazer more like Joe or Jamie?

"Oh, em, more like Joe I think, Jamie's bit more head strong, leaping to the Doctor's defence, I'd rather laugh my way out of trouble, but Jamie would more than likely jump on the baddy and clock him one. Joe was a bit of thinker."

And killed off screen!

"Yeah, killed in a car crash in Spain."

Would you have gone back?

"Yes, totally. I'd left again, I had remarried and had a stud farm and wanted to concentrate on that, but said, hey, if there's a funeral or marriage or something I'd definitely be there for that, even if I'm in Hollywood I'd fly back for that, but new producers came in and asked me back, but I couldn't so they said, "look, we're going to kill him off," but I asked, "please don't kill him, because future producers might want to use him…" But the fan club, God bless them, are trying to get him back as a long lost brother, or maybe he wasn't in the car…"

It's the vogue, it seems, for old characters coming back.

"Yes, absolutely, I'd've done that"

Back to Who, though - why are you always so enthusiastic about it and happy to be associated with it?

"It was three of the happiest years of my life playing Jamie in *Doctor Who*. And then I did 'The Five Doctors' and 'The Two Doctors' – and then I was kicking myself, because I'd just done that, then pantomime, then going back up to *Emmerdale*, but Colin and I had had so much fun doing that, and got on so well together – ganging up on Patrick a couple of times – and I'd've loved to have stayed and gone on with Colin, and I spoke to JNT about that, but I was too busy, but it would have been great."

At last you've managed that with Big Finish, working with Colin in a series of very special adventures. How was that?

"Oh, great fun. Working with Colin the years just roll back. He gets in that booth, and I do, and away we go. He works very similar, in *Doctor Who*, as Pat did, with a "Oh, very well, Jamie, if you must you must, get on with it…" (A passable Colin Baker floats across the table to me).

What about the fan rumour of his appearance in the Matt Smith series?

"Yes, I'm aware of that, but I've never been asked. I keep my fingers crossed every time the phone rings, maybe it'll be Steven Moffat."

Obviously Sarah Jane has gone back – would Jamie be the next logical choice?

"Well obviously, I still look good in a kilt! I still have my figure and all my hair. It's not as if I'm bald and have a big beer belly or anything, it'd be a bit embarrassing if Jamie was, you know, 18 stone and bald!"

Although that might be good character development! Maybe he has his memory back.

"I've always had this idea that the Doctor lands in Scotland and sees this old Highlander, and their eyes meet and we see flash backs of Pat and Jon and everyone and it turns out my memory wasn't even wiped – that the Doctor taught Jamie how to block it from the Time Lords, shut my brain down, and I'm terrified because I can't tell anyone what I've seen, from electric lights to flying beasties, because no one will believe me and I'll be burnt as a witch. So it would be marvellous!"

Are you aware of the hidden season 6b featuring Jamie and the second Doctor? (he's not, so I explain in some detail!)

"Really? Brilliant! Send this interview to Steven Moffat!!!"

It's on its way! Do you like the new series?

"I've dipped in and out of the Tennant stuff, but I've been doing theatre, so I've missed a lot of it. I go on stage at 7 o'clock..."

And also there's the autobiography.

"Yes, we decided to bring it out in January rather than December so it was tarred as a Christmas book – everyone would buy it then, and not at any other time – bring it out now and hopefully it will sell throughout the year. It's called "Hines Sight". You can get it at Frazerhines.co.uk and on Amazon. It's interesting, and we've had a couple of fantastic reviews, because we don't just do a 'what I did next' and we don't dwell just on *Doctor Who* and *Emmerdale*, because let's face it in an autobiography, you want just that, an autobiography."

So what does the future hold?

""I'd like to win the lottery, then I can move to Scotland and visit all my friends! I'm missing a Glasgow convention to go to a wedding in Spain, which is a pity. I'd rather come to Glasgow.

"I'm off to Los Angeles next week for a convention – and then I've had to turn down a musical because there's a couple of tv things in the offing that people have put me up for, so it's important to take a job not just for the sake of working, and regret it. So I'm waiting on the phone to ring."

"I have happy memories. It's like *Doctor Who* – people ask me why I remember it so clearly from so long ago. I think the brain remembers happy times, and that was such a happy time. Patrick and I didn't have one cross word, not in all that time. I never feared he'd come in in a mood, or on the sauce, or anything, it was a glorious time. We'd come to work every day and have a fabulous time. *Doctor Who* was that to me. I used to watch *Doctor Who* when Maureen O'Brien was on it because I used to fancy her, and I always wished I was on it, because then I could work with her. But when I did get on it, it was better."

Deborah Watling

Of course the Doctor is nothing without his female sidekick. Deborah Watling discussed with me the role of Victoria Waterfield.

How did you get the part?

"Innes Lloyd, the then producer, he saw me on a programme called *Alice*[xxi], and I found myself on the front of the 'Radio Times'[xxii], joy of joy, so he watched me and thought it would be rather good if I could play Victoria, so I went up to see him, and we got on very well and one day, about a year later, he rang my agent thinking the time was right, so I went in to have another chat and he said the part's yours! I was like 'Wow!'"

What was that like? The show was as huge then as it is now... was it a massive step?

"It was and is! But then it was a children's programme though, for a half hour on a Saturday at five o'clock, just after the football so I was thrilled because I thought, you know, it's a year's work. And I thought why not. So that's how I found myself on *Doctor Who*."

Where you a fan before you took the part of Victoria?

"No, not really. I saw the very first episode with Hartnell and then I sort of drifted away from it because I was doing my own thing, you know, but when I got the job I thought, hmm, well, I'd better start watching it, so that's what I did."

I know your character was Victorian by era, but do you think the companion reflects the society in which the series finds itself at any particular time? Are they the eyes and voice of the audience?

"Well yes they are, in a way, but the job of the girls, really, was to be the interest for the fathers, quite honestly, and Jamie was the interest for the young women, but I enjoyed Victoria very much and she became a big part of my career. I never thought in those days that the interest would hold up for so long."

Since Susan, Victoria has the best back story, doesn't she? Unlike perhaps Dodo or Polly who preceded her...

"Yes, I suppose she does. She has a family, a home, her father of course... and then the Daleks come in and kill him, they captured me, took me away, and that's how I met the Doctor and Jamie as they came to rescue me."

How were Patrick and Frazer to work with?

"Oh absolutely lovely. I adored them. They made me so welcome immediately, and Pat became sort of like a father, really, but with a mischievous twinkle in his eye, and a great sense of humour, and I could talk to him about anything. One line of mine I just could not get my head round and I said "Pat?" and he'd advise you without being precious because vice versa, sometimes he'd ask me, which is incredibly flattering for a young actress. And he'd ask "Would you like to come and meet my family?" and I said "Yes, of course!" So I met his family, Michael and David, they were around the studio, but then the next week he said "Oh, come and have tea with my family!" and I said, "Again?" and he said "Em, no, another family!" so I did then the next week he said "Come and have tea with my family!" So I said "You have got to be joking!" So he had about three families, that's why he had to keep working. It was very funny."

Do you have a favourite episode of the seven you did?

"I loved the last one, 'Fury from the Deep', and I thought that was wonderful, the monsters were brilliant. You didn't see it for about four episodes, but you knew it was there from the heartbeat! My least favourite was 'Enemy of the World'. I just didn't think it worked. There were no monsters for a start, and I found it a bit lame."

You had a great run, you met all the classics!

"Yeah, I was the companion during the Monster Era! Some of our episodes, like 'Tomb of the Cybermen', I've now seen on the big screen, and they hold up very well. I understand both Ice Warriors and Cybermen have returned with the Great Intelligence recently, so we're going through a renaissance with my old monsters!"

Why did you decide to leave the series?

"Oh well my contract was up and in those days the part that was written, the actual written word, I found I couldn't do much more with.

"I'd tried over the year I was there to make her quite feisty, but I thought, no, I've got to go now, whilst it was still my decision, and Innes Lloyd, bless him, found out, rang me up and said "You can't go! Victoria still has more story lines," but I said "I'm very sorry, I think I have to, really," Which was awful, actually, but I wanted to give myself a chance in the big wide world."

What did you think of your episodes?

"'Evil of the Daleks' – I was quite nervous as it was my first story. I loved the frock, but rushing around in it was hard. The Daleks made me laugh, but the operators were quite strange. They broke the ice though, because one day on set they came up behind me... and I won't tell you what they did with their plungers!

'Tomb of the Cybermen' – Oh yes. Loved this. I think they were my favourite monsters. They were humanoid in form and it was extraordinary the noise that came out of their mouths. It was guttural, terrifying. I thought that story line was brilliant, especially the shot of them defrosting. That was very eerie. I have a lovely character piece with Patrick in this. It's probably my over all favourite scene.

'The Abominable Snowmen' – Oh in windy Wales! With so called monsters the Yeti, but I found them rather cuddly. But it was so cold up there that when we were freezing all the Yetis would circle around me and keep me warm with a hug! And of course my dad was in that, so it was great to work with him.

'The Ice Warriors' – Hmm... I don't remember much about that one. Is that the one with the caves? And dear Bernard Bresslaw[xxiii] chasing us? It was all made of polystyrene, I have to say, and poor Bernie got a move wrong and charged right through the wall! The caves all collapsed! They had to rebuild the set. I mean, it wasn't his fault, he had these Perspex eyes and they'd fog up, so he couldn't see where he was going anyway. He wrecked the set, stood in chaos and turned to me and said "Ere, Debs, was that alright?" Such a funny man.

'Enemy of the World' – lame, I didn't like it. No monsters. Patrick was brilliant though.

'The Web of Fear' - ah yes, of course, Yetis in the underground! I remember we had to ring up the transport people and ask if we could film in the real tube, and they said no, no, no, too dangerous... so we built the set and when it was broadcast there was an awful kerfuffle because the transport people called up furious! They thought we'd filmed there without their permission! It was a very good set. That good that the police thought it was real. This has lasted so long. I understand the Christmas Special is a prequel! So we're not forgotten in the fiftieth celebrations."

The Third Doctor Era

You really believe in a man who has helped to save the world twice, with the power to change his physical appearance? An alien who travels though time and space--in a police box?

As Patrick Troughton bowed out as the Doctor, times were hard for the series.

Tumbling ratings and a disillusioned production team reflected what was becoming a stale and repetitive format. For the series to continue, it needed a new approach, and a brand new look and format.

It helped that the new Doctor's first adventure was produced on film and, as the seventies dawned, in colour for the first time.

But gone was the cosmic hobo wandering through time and space, to be replaced by a velvet-clad dandy, marooned on Earth. The viewers knew a bit of his past - indeed had met his people - and seen the Doctor held accountable for six years of meddling.

On screen and off, things were changing.

Cue, the Master, amongst others…

Jon Pertwee

(interview originally printed in the *Doctor Who* fanzine, *Continuing Mission*, in 1994)

Comic actor Jon Pertwee was a brave choice to take over from the more cosy Doctor of Patrick Troughton and, along with script editor Terrance Dicks and producer Barry Letts, *Doctor Who* would never be the same again.

How did you get the part of the Doctor?

"Doesn't everyone know? Apparently someone else said no, and the next name on the list was me! My agent contacted the *Doctor Who* Production Office just as I was being phoned about the part!"

Did you have to think twice about it?

"I jumped at it! I still do!"

How much of the Doctor is you?

"The mechanics, you see, of acting are different when you take on an iconic role like Sherlock Holmes or Doctor Who. You have to find something that's not on the page to make your version different. With me, I dressed like my grandfather, and asked writers to indulge my love of gadgets. Apart from that, I wanted the Doctor to be as little hard work as possible so I could enjoy the part. So yes, the Doctor is me and I am the Doctor."

Tom Baker says the role is actor proof. Is it?

"It was! We'll never know if it always will be."

Did you have a favourite companion?

"Oh, such an unfair question! As you know I adore Katy and we had and have a very special relationship. I wasn't acting in Green Death. Lethbridge Stewart and I [Nicholas Courtney – Ed] were firm friends, something Terrance Dicks likened to Holmes and Watson, and we loved to cultivate that. Carrie [Caroline John – Ed] and I were much more equals. I don't know if the character worked with the Doctor as well as Katy did, but she was wonderful in the role. And then they decided it was time for women's lib, and Elisabeth [Sladen – Ed] was perfect in that role and went on to be such a wonder with Tom."

So Katy then?

"I also loved Richard Franklin." (he laughs diplomatically)

Do you have a favourite "other" Doctor.

"Well, you know, all the Doctors are the same fella, so if I love one of 'em, I have to love 'em all. So when I say my favourite was the third Doctor that means I really love them all."

Your time was so much more on an ensemble than in previous years. Was this deliberate?

"Well I think Derek Sherwin had a lot to do with the format that Barry Letts and Terrance Dicks were stuck with, but the natural friendship that developed when Katy and Roger (Delgado) came into the team was something that was off screen as well as on. I had no input in that sort of thing, really, as much as one would have wanted it, but the writers seemed to draw from what they saw around them. I wanted a sci-fi James Bond and people drew on that, and I was indulged in my swansong. We had M, Moneypenny and a cinematic baddy."

Why did you decide to leave?

"Well things were coming to their natural end. Roger had died[xxiv], Katy was leaving, the Doctor's raison d'être was changing, so I thought perhaps I'd move on. You see, there isn't much to the Doctor, truth be told, someone like Worzel is a far more layered character, and there's only so many corridors to run around and sonic screwdrivers to fiddle with before it gets repetitive, however much I loved it. I stayed for the team. I'm a great believer in teams. But when Roger died, Katy left, and Barry and Terrance were moving on, it seemed like the right thing to do."

Do you regret it?

"No, I never regret anything. Not so I'd admit it. I'll always be the Doctor. I'm happy to bring him back whenever he's needed."

Do you have a favourite story?

"I loved the Drashigs one[xxv], because I thought they were terrifying. I liked 'The Green Death' but it was a sad ending. Roger's first ('Terror of the Autons') thrilled me. You see, we were criticised a lot for scaring the kiddies, but *Doctor Who* works best when it's up your street, not on an alien planet, because, we've all been up our own streets, and none of us, except Doctor Who, has been on an alien planet!"

Richard Franklin

One of *Doctor Who*'s stalwarts during this time was Richard Franklin's Captain Mike Yates of UNIT. We spoke to him on his return to *Who* in the Paul Magrs audio series, 'Hornets Nest', with Tom Baker as the Doctor:

Richard Franklin is everything you'd imagine he is. Charming, urbane, courteous and quick, with a keen mind and an undying enthusiasm and love for the series he was so much a part of. As one of, arguably, the first characters to have a proper beginning-to-end arc, it was thrilling that he got to make a return; older, wiser but no less exasperated as UNIT's older brother in the family that never dies.

What made you want to change career to be an actor…?

"Well a flash of light! A career path I decided I would like to follow, a road that led me to places I, well, just feel that I wanted to go, things I wanted to do."

And what about Doctor Who? *How did that come along?*

"Well it was fabulous and of course I was very grateful that a) it was an acting job, b) it was television - and of course in one of the most popular series of its day. And we were lucky that we became very much a family of actors all with that goal in mind, to do the best we could with the opportunity we had presented to us and to enjoy doing it."

The "family" atmosphere of the Pertwee-era is legendary… what was it like being part of that?

"Great fun as I say it did feel like a family - all committed to the best we could make it."

What are your memories of your time on Who? *You joined at the same time as Roger Delgado and Katy Manning, with whom (as Jo Grant) Mike was supposed to be romantically evolved.*

"Well, again - I feel that *Who* back then dealt with contemporary issues at the time like ecology, healthy eating etc but subtly trying not to be preaching a message. The romance was never allowed to be more than a friendship and much of that was to do with the BBC or the programme's own sense of not portraying an out and out relationship as such."

What did you think of Jon's portrayal of the Doctor?

"Excellent, of course, and very much a part of the audience's willingness to accept an older, grey haired actor in the role unlike maybe today with its youth orientated culture… I dunno if that would be as accepted today. The series then was of its age maybe."

Was there an 'actor' hierarchy similar to the military one you were in… i.e., was Nicholas Courtney the boss, then you, then John Levene…? Nicholas recounts a tale of real soldiers being a little cautious around his Brigadier. Did you find that too?

"Oh yes! Any two actors in any roles do feel that as part of the portrayal that reverence should be paid to the structure required by the script and as I say we were an ensemble and we did very much feel that we had a duty to fans and to ourselves to make it believable, and portray that realism as best we could - the army ranking system is clearly laid out and yes it does help to bear that in mind when acting etc."

Terrance Dicks talks of the 'natural end' to the UNIT era. With Roger sadly dying, and Jon and Katy moving on, Barry and he too decided to call it a day. Were the UNIT boys part of that - was it an ensemble, mass decision?

"Yes indeed - end of an era - and UNIT was part of that. Doctors and fans move on ... and it wouldn't be quite the same, so maybe yes a natural progression."

Have you seen any of the new UNIT officers in the new series? What do you think of them?

"Can't really comment – haven't seen much of them. But it's nice that they are still there I suppose."

They are a lot more militaristic - but maybe that's in keeping with the times we live in?

"Again haven't seen it much but an interesting point."

You went on to be a director of note after Who... which do you prefer, acting or directing?

"Oh, the opportunities are there to take. Directing is great but the rep theatres are not as widespread as the once were, sadly. They're very much the bread and butter of theatre work etc, but whatever comes, you strive to do the best you can. Each is different and has different challenges."

You always seem enthusiastic with fans and satellite projects like Reeltime and Big Finish; did you realise at the time that your own UNIT triumvirate would be so fondly regarded? How do you find fandom and the enthusiasm of the people around the programme?

"Oh, very much so! Fans are committed to the series are always pleasant and extremely knowledgeable. We loved doing the show, they loved watching it. It's very much a case of what an actor strives to do - please the viewers, the fans who make the programme live on. There's always a few that can turn nasty but they are far outweighed by the positives, we all have a part to play in making it what we want it to be."

And now you're starring in the new 'Hornet's Nest' series... how did that come about?

"Oh, a call offering the part, and I didn't hesitate."

Have you approached Mike differently now? How has he evolved? I described you in my review of 'The Stuff of Nightmares' as Watson to Tom's Holmes... How was it working with the legend that is Tom Baker?

"Oh, fantastic - Tom is such a character and very amusing, and great fun to work with. As for how to approach Mike, well, the script does denote the direction but it did feel like a continuation. Great fun."

Now you've got a taste for Mike again, would you reprise him again? Maybe on the new series?

"Oh, yes, I would love to if offered, who wouldn't?"

Fans do like to see older characters in cameos - the Brigadier in The Sarah Jane Adventures, *for instance).*

"Well, you know, I was not actually in 'The Five Doctors' at first. They hadn't written me a part. But due to fans from Darlington and their persistence writing to the show and pleading for Mike to appear they wrote him into it. So there's always hope."

What do you think of the series now, compared with your time? And the choice of Doctors? The Eleventh Doctor is very young compared with Jon or Tom.

"Can't really comment on the new chap - haven't seen him - but loved Christopher Eccleston. Sad he only did the one series, I would have liked to see how his lonely Doctor character had evolved."

Twelve months isn't perhaps really long enough to maybe establish a role - and each actor must put some of his own stamp on that. Did you agree?

"Oh, yes, indeed, all different aspects of one character... all unique etc..."

Katy Manning

Of course, we can't discuss the Third Doctor without a word or two from Jo Grant herself, Miss Katy Manning, who spoke to me briefly about Jo through the ages.

"It is impossible to describe the difference between working with Matt and Jon. Suffice to say both bought such creative interpretations to the character of the Doctor and both are such generous actors from very different acting backgrounds.

"Three years I worked with Jon every day and I only spent two days with Matt so it's hard to compare them! I do know Jon would have given Matt the Pertwee seal of approval.

"As with the Doctors I believe the companions have all complimented their Doctors brilliantly. Every Morecombe needs a Wise! In my case I was there to ask questions young viewers wanted to (all that science babble), disobey orders, and to help create danger! Jo was totally loyal to her Doctor and in her case to the point of offering her life for his.

"The Doctor needs someone to protect, someone to react to the monsters and someone to banter with and of course someone to save. Jo grew from a nineteen year old innocent to a free thinking adventurer! The character even worked brilliantly years later when I met the wonderful Liz Sladen forty years on! Lucky, lucky me and I loved every moment of it all."

The Fourth Doctor Era

You may be a doctor. But I'm the Doctor. The definite article, you might say.

No one could replace from the hugely successful Pertwee era team. The Brigadier, Third Doctor, Jo, the Master and UNIT, ably backed up by a team of writers including Malcolm Hulke, Terrance Dicks, Bob Baker & Dave Martin - and in Barry Letts a producer who knew the programme like no other and saved it from the doldrums. It couldn't get better... could it?

Step forward builder Tom Baker, Liverpudlian bit part actress Elisabeth Sladen, erstwhile writer Bob Holmes and brand new, first time producer, Philip Hinchcliffe.

Tom Baker

Sometimes, the word 'icon' just doesn't do people justice. When relative unknown Tom Baker took over from the stellar success of Jon Pertwee in the mid 70s, no one – least of all Tom – knew what was about to happen. Not only was lightning caught in a bottle, but the most iconic (that useless, ineffective word again), memorable and beloved Doctor was born, with his jelly babies, scarf, shock of curly hair and beaming smile. Tom created a distant, but friendly Doctor, a man clearly from a different planet and who you could actually believe gave monsters nightmares.

To the general public, even today, Tom Baker *is* the Doctor. Even David Tennant tells tales of being spellbound by this man, whose mind doesn't appear quite to work like that of the rest of us. He's witty, eccentric, moody and clever. People tell tales of him being a genius to work with and equally a nightmare to be around. But one thing is certain, Tom Baker was, for a generation and well beyond, a Doctor of status, and each of the Doctors afterwards are measured against the standards he set for the programme he loved so much that he never really left. Tom lived and breathed the Doctor, being him off camera for millions of adoring children, even marrying a companion as the lines began to blur.

When he left he looked exhausted, the Doctor had him spent, and it was decades before he spoke a word in the Doctor's voice again (we *do not* count 'Dimensions In Time'). Tom was famous for deliberately steering away from *Who*, refusing reunions and Big Finish offers, but he unexpectedly returned to *Doctor Who* for the Paul Magrs scripted BBC Audio series, 'Hornet's Nest' in September 2009.

What brought you back to the Doctor Who *fold?*

"The BBC got me at a good moment about a year ago in a restaurant in Soho. So when the script arrived I was in the mood to accept…"

And how easy was it becoming the Doctor again?

"Very easy and I'll say why. I never thought of Doctor Who as an acting role. It was just ME. Just Tom, being Tom. The hero always wins, so it's all very predictable. So how to be inventive within that predictability is where the fun lies."

Was the obvious quality of Paul Magrs's story a factor?

"Yes, to an extent. But I always feel I can do my stuff and my TURN and make something of anything."

Pairing Tom with Richard Franklin was an unusual step, when perhaps Lis Sladen or Louise Jameson would have made more sense… how did that happen?

"I don't know Richard Franklin… The first plan was that the incomparable Nick Courtney was to be in it. As you know he was unwell at the time of the first recording and had to drop out. Richard Franklin was invited to replace Nick."

The story ['Hornet's Nest'] is a wonderfully potty concept… just up your street?

"You may think the story is potty, I don't find it very odd. I find real life utterly potty and feel we are governed by madmen. I don't mean the present gang anymore than the last lot or any lot. At the moment I'm re-writing the *Bible*. Not all of it. But the Old Testament is a scream and

63

much more gripping than most of the classical myths. So yes, what's potty is right up my street. *Macbeth* was also right up my street."

I can't go on without asking, now you've got a taste of it, will we get more from the Fourth Doctor? Maybe on the telly?

"It would be a backward step to get an old boy to play the Doctor now. I'm not in a state of red alert."

What about with Big Finish then? A kind of full cast adventure?

"That is more like it! I'll see how Hornets buzzes along. And I'm sure I'll get on with Nick Briggs. I also think the series could be done on the radio say five nights a week!"

Is your approach to audio different from that of TV?

"My approach is no different. I really adored doing the 'Hornets'. To be with a group of actors is often very good fun. If it's not fun I'm inclined to walk away and take my dog for a work - I mean a *walk* - or watch Bella the kitten catching flies."

Do you think the BBC will do more? And maybe more importantly, will you he be involved?

"The BBC can do what it likes and if they tempt me I'll probably yield."

What about writing one? You have form, with the self penned 'Dr Who Vs Scratchman' in the seventies.

"Why not? But not everyone agrees with what I like."

What about the rumours of him coming back to Doctor Who *in the new series — even as a hologram as some would have it.*

"Don't know, but I love rumours. I've started a few myself."

What do you think of the actors who had followed him in the role?

"I didn't watch the programme when I was in it. So after I left I lost the urge to see what other chaps were up to."

And of course there are always more rumours of the multi Doctor adventure? The one Colin Baker said was "tosh"

"Did Colin really say "Tosh?" (yes he did. - Ed) I'm game to weigh up anything, you know. I was asked to play God last week in Barcelona, a pilot for a comedy series. Three characters, God, The Devil and the Virgin. Well I'm through with God, I think He's a terrible show off. But I was willing to give the Devil an airing and more than willing to have a bash at the Virgin. I said no."

I'm a fan of your book The Boy Who Kicked Pigs- *have you any more fables in him?*

"Funny you say that. I was writing something yesterday called 'The Boy who Kidnapped God'. I might also air a short story on my website. It's called 'The Watcher'."

So does 'Tom Baker' have a 'typical' day? What would that be?

"A dog lover does have a routine. I'm out every morning and I mean every morning at first light. We have some woodland which is wonderful for Poppy and for me because I can exercise the dog and myself for a couple of hours without having to get dressed. So I either work on my wigwams or have fires. I love lighting fires; the smell of bonfires makes me so nostalgic. My first girlfriend smelled of bonfires so whenever I spark up in the woods I think Doreen. Lawks, I could weep at the thought, she was a whore, she certainly could light a chap's fire, and she did. Do you know what she would do...oh, I won't go on because you just would not believe it."

When you took over from Jon Pertwee in the role of the Doctor, did you have any conception that all this time later that not only would you still be talking about it, but still be playing the character?

"No."

Famously a lot of people (including Mary Tamm, who we spoke to recently) says the Doctor and Tom are almost interchangeable... was that a conscious effort to play him like that or was it worked out with Barry Letts, Terrance Dicks, Philip Hinchcliffe and Bob Holmes?

"It was all my own work, and Barry and Bob Holmes liked it so I carried on. By the time Philip arrived, he also liked it."

After being able to look at your performances through DVDs and commentaries, what are your his thoughts on the role in retrospect?

"The Doctor was the best job I ever had, the one true success in my career."

I think most Who fans would consider the Hinchcliffe/Holmes Era as a Golden Age for Doctor Who. *Were you aware at the time it was creating an iconography of its own?*

"No. We were just working hard to make the series fun for the fans and for us too."

And in the 'middle section' — the Williams Era — you did seem very relaxed in the role. Were you?

"I don't recall being more relaxed. Graham Williams, who was one of the sweetest men who ever drew breath, found me a handful. I got very touchy about some things and there was tension."

And of course, in the final years of your reign, the JNT-era — you seemed very subdued. Were you? If so, why?

"By the time JNT took charge I was pretty well fixed in my approach and I did not like JNT's ideas at all. When I offered my resignation it was accepted like a shot."

The Fourth Doctor had some very memorable companions — Sarah Jane, Harry Sullivan, Leela and two Romanas, not to mention the three 'kids' at the very end — Adric, Nyssa and Tegan. And, of course, there was K9! Who did you think worked best with your particular Doctor?

"I hope they all enjoyed working with me. But by JNT's time my disaffection must have been evident."

An odd question now, but one I'm curious to know the answer to. Tom Baker as a product is iconic, and now seems to be employed because of that iconography … the voice, the walk, the mannerisms, in things like Little Britain *and* Randall & Hopkirk (Deceased). *What's it like looking out of Tom Baker's eyes? Being known for that?*

"What you see is what I am. I have been employed for years by the children who watched me and later went into TV or advertising or radio."

What does the future hold for Tom Baker?

"I had my palm read recently, twenty quid a palm plus VAT. The medium was very emotional and after a swift glance she gave me my money back with tears in her eyes."

And of course, does he have a message for his fans?

"Best Wishes from Tom. Camber Sands, Sussex 2009. September 16th. I think it's the feast of St Gorgonzola, virgin and mystic. She was a very holy one who took a vow never to wash. She kept her vow and lived to a very ripe old age. The cheese was named after her."

Bob Baker

Bob Baker was one half of a writing team during Doctor Who's first Golden Age. You may not know it, but he is responsible for some of the most iconic moments in the series history.

He wrote dialogue that people are still quoting today: "So, you are my replacements, eh? A dandy and a clown!", "Eldrad must live" and "contact has been made" are just three very, very recognisable lines carved deep in *Doctor Who* lore.

Add to that the names of his adventures... 'The Claws of Axos', 'The Mutants', 'The Three Doctors', 'The Sontaran Experiment', 'The Hand of Fear', 'The Invisible Enemy' and 'The Armageddon Factor', not to forget 'Nightmare of Eden' and you can see, this man, along with his writing partner Dave Martin, is a legend in the field.

And of course, let's not forget his career beyond *Doctor Who*. Dabbling with Oscars with *Wallace & Gromit* and writing for other television icons like *Shoestring* and *Bergerac* doesn't even scratch the surface.

But it is for a certain tin dog - one whose charms still delight children today - that he is arguably best known. From a bit part in 'The Invisible Enemy', K9 has become as iconic as the series which spawned him, and, still today, supplies punch-the-air moments with memorable appearances in 'School Reunion', 'Journey's End' and, of course, *The Sarah Jane Adventures*.

How did you get into writing?

"I was making animated films and working with other people who used my animation rostrum (Laurie Booth was one of them), one person was doing a film based on the poem 'Peter Grimes'[xxvi] and I thought he wasn't treating the subject properly so I decided to do it as a movie, but I had not written anything before.

How did you end up working with Dave Martin?

"I met Dave through a mutual friend. He was an advertising copy writer of some note, winning prizes etc. I told him about the 'Peter Grimes' thing and he said 'well let's write it'. So we did, and it very nearly *was* made as a movie. Everything was in place - and the director died. The house of cards that is a movie set-up fell. Dave and I felt that having come so close we'd keep going. He gave up his job and we just wrote things on spec. We got a half hour drama with HTV[xxvii]. Seeing our names on screen was the final push to seeing ourselves as professional writers."

Is there a difference between writing alone and writing with a partner?

"It's not quite so much fun writing alone, but it doesn't worry me."

How did you get your initial Doctor Who *gig, 'The Claws of Axos'?*

"Dave and I sent a script (an army story) to BBC London and a year later we were contacted by a producer and script editor who said they liked it and wanted to do it. We went to see them and gradually, through a liquid lunch, they revealed that they did *Doctor Who* and would we like to do one? We said yes, still confused about our army story. It was only an excuse to meet us incognito to assess us for *Who*. It then took a whole year before our outline was accepted."

What was your thinking behind this adventure?

"We wanted to do a nice kind monster that got to earth to trade (after all that's what we humans did when we crossed the oceans) but then they turn into monsters and threaten the earth. The ship was constructed like a brain so that the Axons were all part of one being."

With 'The Mutants' there was a strong anti-apartheid message – was this deliberate?

"It most certainly was. The idea centred around Britain's slow retreat from Empire after the Second World War. We also played with the idea that not all beings have the same rate of ageing."

And of course being given 'The Three Doctors' must have been a treat! Did you have to research the other Doctors? How much was "given" to you by Terrance?

"Yes. It was great. I'd seen pretty well every *Doctor Who* since it started so I was quite clued up on the others. Dave obviously knew enough to get them in character. Terrance was most helpful at the second draft stage especially after Will Hartnell had to curtail his appearance. Otherwise it was pretty much our brain child, the black hole and all. We bought a load of scientific books to research it all, but it rarely appears on the screen."

'The Sontaran Experiment' is a brilliant little nugget of Who *– how did that come about?*

"It came about because of budgetary constraints, the design budget for a previous show had gone over, with a superb but very expensive set. So the production office decided to make the set economical by doing six episodes with it instead of four; that left two slots empty. We had real fun doing a two-parter who completely on location."

Another classic in so much as you wrote out Sarah Jane is 'The Hand of Fear'. Was the focusing of Sarah in this adventure deliberate seeing as how she was leaving?

"I think you can only say that in hindsight. We just wanted to do a good story based around *The Hands of Orlac*[xxviii], a thirties horror movie. We didn't know Sarah was leaving when we wrote it. I think it worked very well as her swansong.

And then came 'The Invisible Enemy' and a certain tin dog... how orchestrated was K9? I know he joined the TARDIS quite late on, but did you see the potential at the time?

"K9 was entirely un-orchestrated, he was simply a character we put in for to build up the character of the dog loving Professor Marius. We had no idea whatsoever that the mutt would be taken on as a regular. That was a most pleasant surprise."

'Underworld' again has quite strong themes in it – is this something that's conscious in your writing? It's famous for some spectacularly dodgy Blue Screen... how close to your "visions" are the adventures actually realised?

"Dave and I always liked to give a story a strong basis and it was always fun to give an old story – in this case *Jason and the Argonauts* – a sci-fi setting. We made up fun names such as the P7E. Persephone[xxix]. The notable thing about 'Underworld' is that it was almost entirely shot with

CSO, the early version of cgi. It may have seemed 'dodgy' but it was cutting edge at the time. I think the production team always did their best, obviously it wasn't always exactly as we'd envisioned it, but who cares, if the story works it doesn't matter that much."

'The Armageddon Factor' seems to be a story full of strings to tie up – were you given a shopping list? And of course, the Doctor is given a nickname in this – where you aware this was a first?

"Yes, it was the last of the 'Key to Time' story arc, but we didn't let it deter us from doing the story we wanted to do, about a war that might go on forever and a mind set (the Marshall's) that can only see war as a solution. The main thrust was the fact that the final piece to the 'key' was a human being also gave it an edge, in that the Doctor has to decide to end her life to complete the key, a typical Whovian dilemma. No, we were unaware that the Doctor hadn't been given a nickname."

After 'Nightmare Of Eden' you didn't write for Doctor Who again – how come? Of course, a good way back would have been 'K9 & Company', which went to Terance Dudley...Why did they not come to you and Dave? And what did you think of 'A Girls Best Friend'?

"I was never asked to write for it again. Terrence Dudley was a friend of the producer. Dave and I felt insulted that we weren't at least asked to do the 'K9 and Company' script. It turned out to be, in our opinion, very weak, not least because of K9's ungainly movement and being carried everywhere. It was then I knew that K9 had to hover."

Jumping forward a bit, you're now very well known for writing the Wallace and Gromit *stories – how did that come about?*

"I'd known Aardman since they set up in Bristol and greatly admired their work. The BBC wanted Nick Park to do a follow up to 'A Grand Day Out' and felt he might need the help of a writer. I was asked if I'd like to have a go. I met with Nick, we got on well and shared a similar sense of humour – so important when writing in collaboration. The result was 'The Wrong Trousers' and the rest followed on."

And of course then K9 reappeared in 'School Reunion' – were you contacted about that? How does it work with you and the rights to K9 and his appearances in Doctor Who *and* Sarah Jane?
"Russell T. Davies and Julie Gardner asked us if they could use K9 in an upcoming series of *Doctor Who*. We were quite happy for them to do so. It was for a straight forward fee, the same with *The Sarah Jane Adventures*.

And now he's back in his own series – what can you tell us about this? For instance, for Who fans, things like timelines are important – which K9 is this? A new one? One of the two on Gallifrey?

"The regenerated K9 is possibly the one that Leela had on Gallifrey."

Is Doctor Who *implied in any way in the new series?*

"Because of copyrights etc, we were not allowed to link the new K9 to anything in *Doctor Who*. Not even implied, but I think fans will understand some of the cyphers buried deep in the series."

What are you hoping for with it?

"A huge worldwide success and a UK terrestrial showing!"

How important was it to have John Leeson on board?

"John was my first choice but I had to fight for him. I'm really pleased he's doing it."

I then spoke to Bob Baker specifically about the DVD release of 'Underworld'. Dave Martin talks about a specific strategy in pitching 'Underworld' – giving the producers what they wanted with stories. How did it come about?

"I don't recall a 'specific strategy' (unless in hindsight!) It was again, 'Boys, come up with a story that doesn't cost too much.' A usual refrain from the *Doctor Who* office. Dave and I thought over the Greek Odyssey idea after seeing – oh the Italian movie with the fighting skeletons[xxx], combined with an article in *Scientific American* about the possible future of gene banks. The endless journey was sort of a recurring idea in our work (I recall an outline called "The Road " which was exactly like the current one – only with a better, even more depressing ending, along the lines of *Soylent Green*[xxxi]) Of course 'Underworld' was discussed with Bob Holmes before he let us loose on the story"

How did you find the change in producers – you'd worked with Barry, Philip and Graham – or was it more the script editors that helped mould the story? How important is that relationship? Both between script editor and writer and writer and producer?

"It was super going with Philip, since we'd known him from his ITV days. We got on well with Barry. We found Graham was quite enthusiastic for our mad ideas! We got on very well with Terrance, there was a sort of schoolteacher and pupil feeling at first, since he'd guided us through our first Whos which caused him, to quote his letter to us, "great angst, requiring plenty of Macon from the BBC bar!" We found in Bob Holmes a good mate and a built a rapport, second to none. All editors and producers of *Who* had our respect for what they achieved on the budgets they were given"

Do you think 'Underworld' gets undue stick? Watching it, I have to say it was a hundred times better than I remembered. The CSO isn't that bad, is it?

"Yes, I do think 'Underworld' gets undue stick. Seeing it again it wasn't half as bad as I thought it was, and the dialogue resembles something like "I Claudius" at times. The CSO even after working in CGI was pretty reasonable and a brave decision to do it by the director. Definitely underrated."

What struck me was the cast – they are almost universally great… how important is it that a cast 'gets' what's going on?

"We had no say in the casting of our stories, but in the main, our characters have been cast with appropriate thought and care, and was occasionally brilliant - as in 'Underworld', a superb cast. With such a cast, the story is clear, disbelief is quickly suspended. The entire piece starts to work on an entirely new plane. Sorry self praise there!"

When you heard about the CSO at the start, did your heart sink?

"When we heard about the CSO we grimaced, but after seeing the recording of episode one, our spirits were raised somewhat. We felt it better to experiment than use weak SFX."

It's fair to say that it's quite a layered tale, with lots of characters and lots of plot. Perhaps too busy? As a classics student I followed it perfectly now, but for your average viewer at that time do you think it was maybe asking too much?

"It is essentially an adventure story – as was *The Odyssey*[xxxii]. It should work on that level – and those that see the lower layers can enjoy that too. It's a pretty energetic story anyway. Like Wallace & Gromit. Kids don't get the allusions to genres and old movies, but they still like the film."

Are there any aspects of the story you see now and think don't work? Or any that do?

"I think the story works well. I can't think of anything too outrageous."

The solid sets are actually very good, aren't they? The P7E for instance is a massive place...

"The P7E was a great piece of design, it was the most used set of course – that how the CSO paid off I guess."

How was Tom by now? There are rumours of unrest, of fights between him and Louise etc? Where you aware of the force of nature he is as you write a story for him?

"Dave and I loved writing for Tom Baker, we could give him complicated exposition speeches or the odd joke and he always said it as we'd heard it in our heads – as partners we would say the lines to each other to clarify and hopefully edit things as much as possible. Working in a barn in South Gloucestershire, Dave and I saw little of what went on at the shop floor level. Louise (who lived next door to me when at Bristol Old Vic) has never mentioned anything. Though you did hear the odd bit of gossip, but that's what it was as far as we were concerned. Gossip."

You also use K9 "properly" – which of course, you above everyone else would know how to. How frustrating was it to see K9 reduced to a "gun" or a quick fix?

"We got very annoyed seeing K9 used simply as a gun. It was irritating that we'd created a real character who could 'out think' the Doctor at times, who was a real godsend for action set pieces (superior tactics) and also for humour. No, K9 was so often wasted, being stuck around in the set for the odd 'Affirmative' and as a piece of artillery. The Doctor of course, disapproved of 'killing'.

Did you think the relationship with the Doctor and Leela worked any better or worse than say, Jo, Sarah or Romana?

"There was a tension between the Doctor and Leela, she wasn't always the obedient servant of the genius master. Less of the "but Doctor?" kind of dialogue. Leela could take care of herself - often to the Doctor's chagrin. I think they worked well as a team and were on a different level to Romana, Jo and Sarah Jane. Not necessarily better, but certainly different."

Was 'Underworld' a frustrating tale? Did it come out as you had imagined?

"'Underworld', apart from a few changes agreed with Bob Holmes, was pretty well as we wrote it. We were, of course, delighted with the P7E set. That helped it become something a bit special. I'm sure they will have used pieces of the set in another *Doctor Who* story some time."

This was the director's first job wasn't it? Do you think controlling Tom, working with such ground breaking effects and pacing the story was a daunting task for him? How do you think he did?

"All praise to the Director. He chose a rocky path for his first show, but I think he pulled it off brilliantly and we can look back on it knowing that ground was broken on this show – as you said seeing it again after so many years it looks pretty damn good! From the feel and pace of the story I guess he must have controlled Tom, despite being a 'rookie' director. All in all I think this is one of our better ones. And that's a lot down to the director."

Tom Baker Redux
Discussing 'The Horns of Nimon' DVD

The final piece [in the *Myths and Legends* box set] is the 'Horns of Nimon', based on the planet Skonnos and wrapped around a Minotaur legend.

People are either going to love this or hate it. It all depends on where you get your appetite for *Doctor Who* from. If you like serious, reflective and dark, forget it. If you like Tom Baker playing with the biggest toyset in the universe and encouraging others to do the same, then you'll love it.

This is an episode where nothing is small. Tom is beyond out of control, his Doctor is almost manic most of the time, and he sits and waits on cues "live" on camera. Or perhaps this is the genius that Tom brings to the role. He's clearly having a ball. And, if you join in, so will you.

An almost unrecognisable Graham Crowden is explosive as Soldeed from start to finish. I sense no ill will towards Doctor Who in his waaaaay over the top performance (stand up Paul Darrow), but he is Pantomime Incarnate.

"It was heaven to work with Graham Crowden. We did improvise and did offer Kenny new lines. I remember Graham quoting from *The White Devil*[xxiii] - 'I have caught an everlasting cold.' It is a wonderful line and made even more wonderful when after a tiny pause Graham gave a big SNIFF!

"We adored him. I always felt a deep sympathy for his style. He was wonderful in *Heartbreak House* by G. B. Shaw at the National Theatre and of course he was just sublime as the Player in Tom Stoppard's play

Rosencrantz and Guildenstern are Dead. How I hope he is well and happy. He resembled Alastair Sim[xxxiv] I think."

Director Kenny McBain could have struggled to reign in everyone, but in the end allows them carte blanche, even adding his own anarchy with some whistles and bangs as the TARDIS console explodes.

"I seem to remember that Kenny McBain enjoyed the piece; we certainly did. Kenny was quite slight physically. He was not at all slight in any other way. I got on well with Kenny. Looking back I got on reasonably with nearly all of them."

But was the absurdity of the story relevant to his own performance? The dafter, the better?

"The absurdity of the stories never bothered me at all. I was brought up as a Roman Catholic in Liverpool so I grew up steeped in absurdity. I still am. I find most of life utterly absurd. And what seemed important years ago now seems to me to be farcical. There seems, to me, no meaning. The pains and pleasures were all real but meaning? Oh, no."

And of course, script editor Douglas Adams would have something to do with that absurdity?

"Douglas Adams compelled affection. We loved him and he loved us. I was very amused by his sense of the ABSURD! There we go again! I was deeply grieved when Douglas died. I'm grieved right now to think of him."

There were rumours of a tumultuous rehearsal period during this time...

"The rehearsals may have been tumultuous. I liked Tumult. I cared about making the story interesting for our fans."

And he cares about the fans too, that much is obvious...

"I still love the fans and often go out to meet them. When I'm in Soho where there is a great deal of new building going on, the scaffolders yell out "Aye aye, Doctor." and I yell back and people on the pavement look amazed and then THEY recognise me and sometimes tell me sweet things as the memories of long ago come swirling back".

Tom also has a lot of nice things to say about John Leeson and K9.

"David Brierley was perfectly competent as K9 but he was not in the same league as John Leeson, whose work in rehearsal was sometimes miraculous. The BBC was committed to their version of the Robot Dog and did not see the genius, yes, the sweet genius of John's work in the rehearsal room.

"The look on John Leeson's face when the incomparable Myra Francis barked the line "point the Dog at the rock." I wanted to develop it. I thought it would be better if we all looked at each other and someone should say: "What did she say?" And I wanted to say" "She said *point the dog at the rock*!" And then we could all shout together: "POINT THE DOG AT THE ROCK!" (Cue for a song)

"That line became a catchword from that moment on. But there in the rehearsal room we saw the power of a reaction. Barry Letts would have loved that scene. I think Barry Letts would have seen all the possibilities. More sad thoughts! He was very special."

So a great time then, Tom?

"The Doctor was the best part I ever had. Nothing admits of comparison, nothing. I am so grateful to Barry, to Bill Slater and Shaun Sutton and to Ray Harryhausen who directed *The Golden Voyage of Sinbad*[xxxv]."

John Leeson

And of course, we can't talk about K9 without talking to John Leeson, the man who made him real.

I interrupted John's gardening to chat about all things *Doctor Who* – from his early association with the programme to his triumphant, punch-the-air return, and his increasingly starring role in *The Sarah Jane Adventures*. We even managed to chat about the then new K9 series.

Looking at your CV is an impressive job – I didn't know you'd played Bungle in Rainbow *for instance! And* Dad's Army *too!*

"Given that I started out in 1964 following a training at RADA, I seem to have covered many bases including several years as a character actor in repertory theatre; an amazing time as a supporting actor during the 'seventies and early 'eighties in what I call 'the golden age of TV sitcom'; a clutch of West End productions, and a parallel career in voiceovers and television presentation including TV commercials, I'm just thankful that the 'phone has rung for me from time to time across all those years."

What made you want to become an actor?

"Now that simple question begs a rather complicated answer in my own case: There are in my view two kinds of actor: those who are natural 'displayers' and those who are natural 'hiders'. I think I come squarely into the second category as someone who is keen to 'submerge' into a character rather than to strut my stuff. For me, acting provided initially a means of escape from the dilemmas of the real world, until I discovered (very quickly) how the business of acting brought one squarely up against them….and then some! So, possibly, acting is a means of 'problem solving' on behalf of whatever character I am playing. Arguably, this is fun!"

And of course then came 'The Invisible Enemy' and a certain tin dog… how did that come about? Was it always going to become a recurring role?

"My engagement in *Doctor Who* as K9 (and the voice of a large prawn-like creature called the Virus of the Swarm) was as a result of a chance meeting with a director friend of mine who knew I was not averse to earning my crust in offbeat ways (Bungle Bear in the original series of *Rainbow*, for example). He introduced me to Graham Williams, at that time the producer of *Doctor Who*, and the commission to voice K9 followed. At the time of my initial engagement K9's character was due to appear in just one storyline, but during the course of rehearsals the BBC decided that there was enough mileage in K9 to have him appear subsequently as a regular companion."

Tom Baker speaks very highly of you. As you know, Tom is bonkers and liable to make stuff up for a laugh. So when he talks of you doing rehearsals and actually playing K9 on all fours, I wonder… apocryphal or true?

"I'm not sure I know that Tom Baker is 'bonkers' – as you suggest – but he was perfectly right to mention that I ran around on all fours in rehearsals 'being' K9. There was a good reason for this, as the physical module of K9 was still being built and finished, and as I was engaged for the production as an actor – not merely a voiceover artist who would otherwise 'phone in' a performance – so I obliged by 'acting' as K9. It may have looked ridiculous to see me scuttling round on all fours, but it gave K9 a vital 'live' dynamic in rehearsal and performance… a quality that has kept the character alive to this day, perhaps, even though I am no longer required to scuttle! The additional benefit to the other actors was that they could see where the real K9 was supposed to be moving to once the 'real' K9 was active on the set."

What's he like to work with? Mary Tamm says infuriating and genius in equal measures.

"I can honestly say that although our own temperaments are possibly 'chalk and cheese' I found Tom one of the most enjoyable actors to work with. He was ideal casting as The Doctor who, for me, has to be an iconoclast, a bohemian wilfully at variance with the strictures of convention, with an effervescent energy both mentally and physically to carry the huge weight of playing a Time Lord. You simply cannot cast a 'suit and tie' actor into such a role – and Tom's phenomenal physical and mental energy allowed him to 'celebrate' the unworldliness of the character he was playing which, as I hope you'll agree, was the hallmark of the 'regeneration' period he occupied."

And of course you had a number of glamorous leading ladies… Louise, Mary and Lalla… oh, and Matthew. How were they to work with? Did they approach working with you – or K9 – differently?

"Hey, didn't I just! I was very lucky indeed to have such wonderful female companions (even though, as K9, viewed at knee-height!) It would be impertinent of me to advance opinions on their different merits because each of them had very distinctive and hugely entertaining offstage personalities. Needless to say their own personalities naturally affected the way they played their characters. It is probably worth remembering that they all had an uphill task when each of them joined the series: the characters were already pre-set by the writers, so each of them would have had to surmount the difficulty of finding their own 'voice' at a very early stage of their engagement....all credit to each of them for having done so. Louise Jameson told me that for her K9 was the next best thing to 'phone a friend'! At least K9 helped Mary Tamm with crosswords, even though he didn't get all the references for the phenomenally cryptic ones Lalla Ward used to sail through!"

Tom is on record as being very frustrated with the prop... where you onset during recordings? How did that go?

"You have to remember that studio time is phenomenally expensive, and that 'the clock is king' when it comes to recording. Yes, indeed, the physical K9 module was SLOW, noisy, underpowered, and therefore subject to frequent breakdowns. No wonder frustrations arose, and not only on Tom's part but mine too! I was on the set and, curiously, feeling embarrassed that the 'other' part of me – the body to my voice- was behaving in such a dysfunctional manner....eating up hugely valuable studio time in running repairs. From time to time this was an embarrassing agony!"

You left the role after the Key To Time (when you appeared onscreen too in 'The Power of Kroll'). What made you want to leave?

"Oh yes, so I did... thanks for reminding me. Bearing in mind the WYSIWYG (*'what you see is what you get'* – Ed) nature of any character in sci-fi or science fantasy (the latter being probably closer to the *Who* genre) I realized quite quickly that in performance terms there was nowhere else for the character to go. He was set. K9 has no emotional life, no inner depths to explore or develop which might enhance his character. He is what the audience sees and expects from him. On the one hand I could sit back and keep taking the BBC-sized paychecks until the character had reached its 'sell-by' date; on the other I could take a risk of staring unemployment in the face in a bid to broaden my acting career in the outside world. This was my choice. I didn't know what lay before me ... possibly months of 'resting' as my face hadn't been around the business for awhile. From the point of view of my own career this move was a 'must'. The rash move paid off - and I can report that having left *Doctor Who* I had one of the busiest years of non-*Who* work I can ever remember!"

Then JNT talked you into coming back...?

"David Brierley, who had succeeded me, decided that for him, one season of playing K9 was enough. As there had been a change of producer in the interim I was prepared to hear arguments why I should return. Briefly, JNT told me that K9 was being run out of the series in a graceful fashion across a few upcoming stories and, as his original voice, would I mind coming back to 'wrap him up' in a decent fashion. I guess I weakened, as I'd enjoyed creating K9's character in the first place, so I returned. In hindsight it seems to have paid dividends, as K9 is still very much alive even now, over thirty years after his initial appearance!"

And suddenly you were getting your own show! How did 'K9 & Company' come about?

"You may remember that Lis Sladen as Sarah-Jane Smith had charge of K9 in 'The Five Doctors', even though K9 himself was kept within the bounds of her own garden fence and not allowed by her to take part in the subsequent adventure. This nexus between the two characters seems to have sparked off the idea for a follow-up series involving Sarah-Jane and K9. 'K9 and Company' never got beyond its pilot episode stage, partly through budgetary restraints (though the initial story was hardly awash with production money), and partly because of a personnel change at the higher levels of BBC production management."

Was filming that different to filming the parent series?

"Location filming is filming, whatever. The story was filmed mostly in darkest Oxfordshire – 'A Girl's Best Friend', as I seem to remember the story was called, turned out to be a somewhat earthbound tale involving covens and witches, rather than anything with an extra-terrestrial fantasy element."

I know you came back to Who specifically to wave goodbye to K9, but if 'K9 & Company' had taken off, would you have stayed with the parent series too? Or was that never an option?

"I don't know the answer to that one. Presumably the *Doctor Who* series would have continued without K9 as he 'left' the series in 'Full Circle', remaining with Romana Two in E-Space. (Memo: wrap up well if you're visiting E-Space, it is beyond very cold!)"

You're famously very enthusiastic about the role and about your association with the programme – more than some others. What's your opinion of fandom and being associated with your vocal work as apposed to your physical presence?

"You are right to credit me with enthusiasm… it is one of the qualities that rubbed off Tom Baker, i.e. the ability to 'celebrate' what you do. This applies right across the board to life in general, of course, not simply to acting. As I mentioned earlier, as a 'hiding' kind of actor I have never sought the kind of recognition accorded to some of my peers who prefer the limelight! I am delighted, of course, to be indulged by fan audiences for having provided a life and soul for a pretty inanimate character, purely in terms of a voice characterization ... and I am sure that were it not for their continued support and enthusiasm for what has turned out to be one of the most iconic series on television, *Doctor Who* wouldn't have made the great leap forward into the 21st Century broadcasting schedules.

"I feel very honoured to have been invited to cross that 'great divide' myself. (How many *Doctor Who* fans did it take to turn on a lightbulb? .... None! They all stood around the lightbulb hoping and praying it would come on again, and after a gap of eighteen years, it lit up again all by itself!)"

You've also come back to Doctor Who *as a Dalek! How did that come about, and how do you approach such a creature? I know some bloke called Nicholas Briggs does all the Daleks now, but, when you did it, you were all specific creatures with an actual hierarchy...?*

"Thanks for the reminder. I'd forgotten. Yes, I think I was the voice of Davros on one occasion – I can't remember when, though."

And you've made a few cameos in the New Series... how was that? I know David (Tennant) bemoaned the fact you weren't there for the filming of 'School Reunion' as he was dying to meet you...

"Given what you say, thank goodness I met him at a *Doctor Who* convention shortly afterwards otherwise he'd probably be dead by now. Now there's a star!

What're the differences with working on the new series compared to the old?

"Given the way you frame your question, I am no longer a required 'live' presence during recordings in the studio complex. Unless they forget me completely there'll usually come a point following the completion of filming when I'll get a call from the post-production supervisor to book me into a dubbing session in London. On one occasion I think they forgot me! However, I have been generously invited to the *Doctor Who* studios on a couple of occasions to provide my own guide track for subsequent ADR (additional dialogue recording) work to follow at a later date."

And of course from that 'School Reunion' appearance came The Sarah Jane Adventures *and a brand new lease of life for K9!*

"I think you'd have to ask Russell T. just when a decision was made to float the 'Sarah Jane' strand."

Were you disappointed not to feature more heavily?

"Not really, no. I am well aware of the physical difficulties K9 has been known to cause in the studio and on location, so I could easily accept a sparing use of his services. You have to remember, too, that copyright in K9 is not owned by the BBC but is vested in the writer Bob Baker (and presumably the estate of his co-writer, the late Dave Martin) from whom permission would have to be sought for his use."

I understand that in the new series however you appear in at least half the stories… That must be fun…? Did you manage to work with David again in his guest starring role?

"Yes and no! It was great sharing a to-and-fro of dialogue with David, but he had already filmed his exciting contribution – and I was voicing K9's responses to his screen presence weeks later, sitting in a dubbing theatre in Soho."

Is K9 appearing in David's swansong? It seems that everyone and their mum is…

"Unless you know something I don't, I don't think so. Mind you, I'm generally the last person to hear anything!"

And now we hear from Bob Baker that you're reprising K9 again in the new Australian show… did that come about?

"By invitation. The Australian version of a K9-led series with an all-singing all-dancing CGI K9 had been talked about for years, and given the lengthy passage of time I'd assumed all the casting (and voice casting) had been sewn up, done and dusted. I thought no more about it until I received a call earlier this summer from Bob Baker's associate, Paul Tams, to inquire if I'd be interested in providing a 'new' voice for a 'new' K9. I guess I must have answered in the affirmative! How could I not?"

I have to tell you everyone we've spoken to is thrilled that YOU'RE doing K9 again. To Who fans, you and that little tin dog are inseparable.

"Well, I'm genuinely delighted, hence, I dare say, the invitation I allude to above."

How different is the new K9 series to the original and of course, K9, who "regenerates" in episode one… we understand from Bob he's a little, em, "trendier" in dialogue. And of course, it proves that K9 Mk1 at least escaped the Time War! Or is it Romana's Mk2?

"I guess you're going to have to wait and see! The Australian series is certainly different, and, as Bob says, K9 is certainly trendier and amazingly more energized than the original. Without breaching the Official Secrets

Act I think I can say that the new series is likely to target the same general market as *Sarah-Jane* ... but as it hasn't even been broadcast in Australia yet I imagine it'll be a while before we get to see it over here assuming a broadcast network picks it up."

What do you have coming up in the future?

"Broad beans, waxy potatoes and courgettes – I just need more sunny days for them to flourish in my garden....but who can beat fresh homegrown veg?"

Do you have a message for the hoards of Doctor Who *fans out there?*

"Imperative you keep the faith!"

You heard it from the tin dog's mouth!

Elisabeth Sladen

But of course, the *Doctor Who* universe is a broad and complicated place, K9 may have been a companion after she left, but quintessential *Who* companion Sarah Jane Smith also had help from the tin dog, both in her initial spin off series (or was that K9's?) *K9 & Company*, and also in the spin off of the spin off which was also a spin off of a new series episode – *The Sarah Jane Adventures*.

Before she died, I spoke to Elisabeth Sladen about *The Sarah Jane Adventures*, her renaissance on *Doctor Who* and her original, classic time on the show.

"I was suddenly very aware that I'd walked in at the end of a party," Elisabeth Sladen said in that breathless, slightly distracted, extraordinarily earnest voice. "Jon Pertwee, who'd approved my appointment, had announced he was leaving, and even though he was welcoming and very professional, I was very aware that I was at the end of something rather than the beginning, because things were very much in flux. It was an unusual feeling because I was very much hoping I was at the start of something brilliant!"

How different was that first season to your next two?

"Oh, chalk and cheese, really. I pretty much stayed true to the brief of Sarah Jane during that time – but then, I say that, but when I think about it, Sarah's brief (the nosey investigative journalist) has stayed the same since that time."

It seemed to me you're more keen to discuss your time with Tom rather than Jon?

"Hmm. Maybe. You know, I've spoken about all of this lots of times. I adored Jon Pertwee. Absolutely adored him. But I always felt that Katy was Jon's girl, and I was Tom's."

You must have been more comfortable with Tom coming in along with Ian Marter as the new boys, when you were the vet?

"Haha! Vet! I'm not sure I'm even that now! Actually, though, I didn't, because I was tying up loose ends with Jon whilst they were getting to know each other. As the new boys on the block, Tom and Ian had bonded before I joined, so, again, I found myself too busy trying to impress then than thinking, yeah, this is easy now. Tom is extraordinary to watch. Just spellbinding."

Why do you think Sarah Jane has endured for so long? Out of all the companions before or since, she's probably the one everyone identifies as a Who *girl.*

"Well to answer that I'd have to accept it! But *if* it's the case, it's probably because I was lucky to be holding onto Tom's coat tails when he really began to fly, along with some amazing scripts and production by Philip Hinchcliffe and Bob Holmes. I was in the right place at the right time."

And, I suggested, perhaps she was very earnest at attacking the role? She didn't seem to see the heroine in distress thing as demeaning her in anyway.

"The role of the companion is to answer questions, react to monsters and get rescued by the Doctor. It's rare, especially back in the day, that we drove any story. When dear Ian left, especially, I was happy to embrace that. You see, if I'm being threatened, or screaming, or hypnotised or in

95

danger, then I'm the centre of the Doctor's attention, and where else would I want to be? I'm much more the protagonist in *The Sarah Jane Adventures*, I fulfil the role of the Doctor, if he's not there, and that is different from being tied to a rail track."

Elisabeth has worked with four Doctors (six, if you count 'The Five Doctors'). Does she have a favourite?

"Each is very different. As an actor, it's an interesting thing to watch. Whilst Jon was very mother-hen, protecting me with his big cloak (itself an odd thing given that initially Sarah would resist that), Tom was deliberately very alien, and he'd more than likely tell Sarah to get on with it and come back when she'd stopped sniffling! With David, his affection for me and the series was clear, and that was wonderful, so flattering, and it made his Doctor, for me, a nostalgic one. Matt had the air of Tom about him – I mean, that line about Katy being baked! Really!"

And a favourite?

"No, not a favourite. But I was Tom's girl. He was naughty, irreverent, he's push the part and I liked that. We'd work out ways to come in a room, adlib naughtily, but busk it so the director wouldn't get annoyed. It didn't always work."

You nearly didn't come back for School Reunion did you?

"I didn't want *Doctor Who* to wheel out its old maiden aunt for a pointless cameo. I'm very protective of Sarah, and I'm so proud of my time on the series with Jon and Tom. I'm very much aware of how much that time means to the fans. I didn't want to just show up, wave and leave. It would have diminished Sarah as a character and undermined her memory. I was so flattered at how Russell and Phil approached the character, though, I was in tears."

Since 1973, Elisabeth Sladen *was* Sarah Jane Smith. This year, 2013, would have seen her fortieth year in the role, but, as we all know, she was sadly taken from us just as *The Sarah Jane Adventures* was hitting its stride.

For a new generation of children, Sarah Jane was a hero. And Elisabeth Sladen showed us that age didn't matter when it came to universal appeal. She was sparkling, brilliant, spectacular. Speaking during the filming of her last season of *The Sarah Jane Adventures*, I asked her one last question, little knowing the resonance it would carry.

Will Sarah Jane ever stop?

"The series? Probably. Everything ends. I'm just enjoying it whilst it's here."

The character?

"Never!" she answers quickly. "Thanks to that Doctor. Sarah is always out there, fighting the fight."

My Sarah Jane, I thought once I heard of her death. Out there. Still.

Mary Tamm

Another wonderful, graceful actress and companion of the fourth Doctor was also taken too soon, and, again, I was lucky enough to catch up with Mary Tamm on the release of her autobiography.

Mary Tamm is *Doctor Who* Royalty. In 1978, Season sixteen took an unusual step away from the Gothic excesses of the Hinchcliffe/Holmes era with a series of linking stories known collectively as *The Key To Time*. Given to the Doctor as a bona fide "assistant" – as apposed to "companions" Sarah and Leela – by The White Guardian, Time Lady Romanadvoratrelunar was haughty, clever, brave and naïve, and, it seemed, more than a match for the reluctant Doctor. Of course, she was played by the spectacular Mary Tamm, who first appeared on screen in a sleek one piece white dress and feather boa raising the temperature for a thousand pre-pubescent fanboys and dads alike. But Romana was more than glamour and looks and Mary Tamm's one season in the TARDIS has stayed in the memory and is thought of, for the most part, with great affection.

You're a graduate of the Royal Academy of Dramatic Art… what made you want to be an actor? Is it in your family?

"Well, to be honest, I have no idea why I wanted to become an actor. I was playing in the street with a little girl and she announced that she was going to be an actress when she grew up, and I thought, wow, maybe I could be one too, and that was that! I was about six at the time......mind you; my mother was an opera singer, so she influenced me in all things cultural, as you will find out when you read my book!"

You began in rep in Birmingham, is this correct? How scary is that first step out onto stage? Do you prefer stage to tv work?

"Yeah, I did, but I was more excited than scared, as I was fulfilling a lifelong ambition, remember. Stage was my passion, and I only fell into films and TV by accident. I still love it, but now prefer working between the two mediums of theatre and celluloid."

You've appeared in a few seminal tv programmes over your career – Coronation Street, The Likely Lads, Brookside *– as well as movies like* The Odessa File. *The list is huge. With regards to joining an established cast, which you sort of did with* Doctor Who *too, is it a different approach than say starting from the beginning of a series?*

"Hmmmm, vastly different - it is terrifying, frankly, to join a British Institution, whereas when you start a series from the beginning, you have a role in its creation. With something like *Who*, or *Corrie*, you are confronted with rigid parameters which you have to fit into.

I understand when you were first offered the role of Doctor Who *you turned it down, not wanting to be another "damsel in distress"… how did the producers convince you?*

"It was not so much the producers as the director and my agent - there is a long story about this question which is answered in the book."
Quick word on the genius of Mr Tom Baker – what's he like to work with? I get reports of everything from genius to infuriating and perhaps everything in between.

"You said it! Tom and I got on very well, eventually, after a rocky start - I still meet him from time to time, and we always have a great laugh together."

How did you approach the role of Romana? Again we hear that time wasn't particularly of the essence. Some others have said "simply say the lines and turn up", but your Romana always seemed to have a keen wit behind her.

"I guess with my classical training and theatre experience, I was able to approach the role intelligently. I was the first companion to have an established career behind her, apart from Louise (*Jamieson, aka Leela – Ed*), who also trained at RADA; some people say we stand out for this reason."

You were of course put in some wonderful costumes in the role. Did you have a favourite? The striking white robes for 'The Ribos Operation' spring to mind. I'm not sure why…

"I helped to design the costume for The Androids of Tara, so this one is my favourite. Over the years I have received more compliments about this costume than any other, although the white dress is copied most by fans that turn up in various versions of it at conventions!"

As a serious, proper and established actor, how different is Doctor Who *to work in? Some suggest its melodrama, but Tom says that if you don't take it seriously you lose the audience. Did you take his lead?*

"Tom took the part very seriously, as did I - he is a consummate professional, and you cannot be anything else to make the part, and therefore the series work - to not take your work seriously is a complete disaster for an actor. Tom was being flippant when he said that, I am sure!"

I love the relationship between Romana and the Doctor. First he's reluctant, then sometimes he's almost teacher-ish, but there's a mutual respect, he allows you to go off and have your own adventure, and, maybe, did I sense a little chemistry?

"Oh very much so, we got on like a house on fire, as we both share a wicked sense of humour!"

How was your other co-star, the fabulous K9, to work with?

"Fabulous is the word - John Leeson was a star!"

And you had some varied locations, from beautiful countryside to difficult swamps...?

"Yes, some locations were very cold, damp and uncomfortable to be in, to be sure, but it is all part of the actor's life! You learn to live with it, and the nicer locations make up for it."

And at the end of that season you decided to leave? Was that a difficult decision? Romana was popular, had a great rapport with the Doctor, were you asked to stay? There's an apocryphal story that you were pregnant...

"NOT TRUE! The story of my being pregnant is a myth, and I have recently edited my Wikipedia page to amend the falsehood. John Nathan-Turner started it, and I was very cross with him about it, the naughty man! My daughter was born in November 1979!

"I decided to leave because the part was not up to what had been promised, and there was nowhere left to go with character."

Did you ever regret leaving? Romana MkII went on to great success with Lalla.

"No, I had done my time, and had some very exciting film work soon after which left me with no regrets, or looking back."

You've returned to the role of Romana in the Big Finish Audios along with Lalla. How was that, working with "another" Romana. Famously, the Doctors were known for getting together during anniversaries etc, but never a companion…

"Yes, well, it was weird, at first, and I felt strongly proprietorial about Romana, so it was strange to hear Lalla doing 'my' part. She is so good in it, however, and we are such good pals that I soon got over it!"

And of course now we have Elisabeth Sladen returning to Doctor Who *and having her own spin-off show! With K9! Would you ever appear in the programme again?*

"Yes, I would love to appear in the programme again, I love the new show and Lis is great in the new spin off series. I could come back as Romana, or play a juicy villainess part!"

What do you think of the new programme in general and its choice of Doctors… there's a lot more, um, kissing now…

"Yes, I find that a little shocking - my view of Time Lords (and ladies) is that they are above that sort of thing, so it is a shame that any hanky panky is going on, in my view - as I said above, I love the new series - Sky TV approached me to do a news interview when the new doc was announced, and I had a few minutes to expand on my ideas as to how a Time Lord should behave, which was fun to do. I think David Tennant is incredible, and am looking forward to Matt's performance now."

A lot of actors complain of typecasting, especially the companions. Did you have any trouble with the direction casting directors wanted to take you after Who? *Did you ever consider doing something radical, like Katy Manning did (she posed nude with a Dalek), to try and "break the mould" of a "Who Girl"? Perhaps a gritty drama or something far removed from the very glamorous image you have?*

"I had a varied and extensively character driven career before *Doctor Who* so was not really affected by any typecasting as such. A lot of people did not even know I had been in the programme, so I had a previous reputation to fall back on. I think, apart from Louise, that *Who* was the first and only claim to fame for many companions, which means that typecasting was more prevalent for them.

"I have broken the glamour mould in many stage productions, notably playing Mari Hoff in *The Rise And Fall Of Little Voice*, a drunken, over the hill mother from hell - about as far removed from Romana as you could imagine!

When looking at your body of work, both before and after Doctor Who, *it strikes me as constant and very diverse... is this a conscious effort to remain "moving" as it were? It looks like there's hardly an established programme you haven't appeared in...*

"Yes, well I am a workaholic, and accept any job that come along, as opposed to choosing roles to fit in with a plan or image - I have no false ideas about stardom or how I am perceived - in other words, I am pretty down to earth and just consider myself as a jobbing actor - I am always grateful for work, no matter what it is!"

What has been the highlight of your acting career?

"I suppose *Brookside* was one, although I feel I have had many...*Brookie* was good for me because the character was developed to become a highly dramatic part and the writers wrote very much for the actors, observing them in the studio and getting ideas for storylines from their (the actors') own lives and circumstances."

Do you ever get fed up with people constantly harking back to that one year of Who *you did?*

"Sometimes, but only a little - I am used to it now and accept , quite happily that *Doctor Who* is one of the great British institutions- so really, I am very proud to be a part of it, and always will be."

Did you know at the time you were joining a very loyal family?

"No, I did not realise the extent of the fan's loyalty, but soon did when I visited the first few fan cons in the States, which I go into in great depth in the second book - i.e. volume two of my autobiography."

Is there any role you haven't yet taken and what like to? (Personally, I'd love to see you as Gertrude in Hamlet. It's made for you!)

"Yes, Dirty Gertie is a great role, as is the Scottish queen and Jocasta - all parts I would love to do one day, plus Medea - I love the Greek plays - the women's parts are superb!"

What do you have coming up in the future?

"I am appearing in *Eastenders* - a really good guest role over four episodes."

Do you have a message for all your fans out there in the world of Doctor Who?

"Hi to all the loyal fans who have kept the show going and, more importantly, moving forward into a new millennium! Buy my book!"

Louise Jamieson

Along with Romana and Sarah Jane, Louise Jameson's savage Leela was another iconic companion and partnership for Tom Baker's Doctor. She spoke to me about her time on the show and her thoughts on the role of the companion.

Was it difficult joining the series?

"Not at all. Pennant was such a good director as far as creating a safe space was concerned and I know he really rated me so I felt quite confident."

I know it's pretty well documented that Tom wasn't keen on a companion and was a little resistant at the beginning.

"Yes that's true, but now we are fine. He didn't like the character of Leela and that overlapped into not liking me very much. But he has been publicly and sincerely apologetic about all that now, and although I never thought I'd be saying it, I adore - absolutely adore - working with him on all the Big Finish stuff. We have eight more stories lined up for this year.

"He's funny, erudite, intelligent, witty, clever, talented - I wish we could have had that bond earlier, and I would have stayed in the job a bit longer, but that's life, and we have what we have now. And if I had stayed I might never have been free for *Tenko* and I wouldn't have missed that for the world..... Nor would I have met the two fathers of my two sons, which is what life is all about really. It's just the way my cookie crumbled."

Leela is a fantastic concept for a companion, you must have seen countless possibilities with her...?

"Yes, I saw more than they did I think.....'Talons' came the closest to exploring the teacher/pupil relationship and the lovely moment when the doctor saw Leela in her full regalia, Victorian costume.... More moments like that would have been fabulous. The Big Finish series of course is all about educating Leela and I think the writers have really flown with it."

Did you think she was treated well by the writers?

"Given the era that they were writing for Leela I think the writers did as well as they did for any companion, if not better actually. Particularly Robert Holmes, closely followed by Chris Boucher. But there was much more to be found. The companions nowadays get a better crack of the whip, but women do in general. Art reflecting life."

Did you buy the Andred/Leela love thing?

"No. Graham sidled up to me the night before we shot the farewell scene and asked me to change my mind. They had deliberately underwritten it in the hopes that I would change my mind and decide to stay. It was all very flattering but I had signed a contract to play Portia at the Bristol Old Vic by then and was ready to leave. I wasn't really happy you know, and it was time to move on."

I know you and Chris Tranchell tried to inject some connection in the relationship in earlier scenes to pre-empt your departure..?

"Yes we did, and he was lovely to work with. It was nobody's fault that the story line was weak, just several people wanting several different things and no one clear focused vision."

Standard question - do you have a favourite story?

"The Sun Makers."

Why?

"It had fantastic political content. Bob Holmes thought it was going to be his last story for the BBC, and he was doing a kind of two fingers to the corporation. I thought the performances were brilliant and brave. Who can forget Henry Wolfe's Inspector?

"Completely invested, from every angle, the design, the script, the performances, the directing. And for once the companion got to drive some of the story. Also Bob gave me some scenes away from Tom to give me a bit of a break. But I must say again that is all over and history and Tom is now just adorable."

You were the companion to the Doctor during what's known as a golden age. Were you aware of the quality of tv that was going out?

"I think I was aware of the quality of work that was happening, but the same was true of theatre too. I had just done a near three year stint with the Royal Shakespeare Company and work was abounding with marvellous rep companies and art centres springing up everywhere. I loved the work all through the 70s and 80s - I really had a blessed time."

How different were Philip Hinchcliffe and Graham Williams to work for?

"Very. Philip was very smooth and sure of himself. Spoke with confidence, worked a lot from the box where they pushed all the buttons. Was there in a crisis. Graham was very hands on, often on the studio floor, gentle conversations with all and sundry, not nearly as tough as Philip."

Did you think that that - what, fourteen months?

"I think it was more like ten."

- of your life would resonate so long in your life. Leela's still very much a part of you now, isn't she?

"Yes weirdly, and that is in no small part thanks to the fans. They have kept the memory of this unique and quirky series going, they have kept the flag flying, they have made being a geek fashionable, and they have brought the show back. Thank you, I sometimes feel very humbled by the loyalty of those who saw me in a show almost forty years ago, a show which still brings me an income, and takes me if not around the universe, then certainly around the world. I am off to Sydney next month, and Chicago later in the year, and last year went to Melbourne and Los Angeles. What a blessing that job was/is."

What was it like returning to the character with Tom?

"Strangely easy. I think the choice of voice rhythm.... not to change 'would not' and 'could not' to 'wouldn't' and 'couldn't'. Once you are speaking in that way, the rest is easy. The Companion Chronicles [from

Big Finish – Ed] really help, and there I was, match fit, once Tom came on the scene."

I know you'd played her for Big Finish before, but did tom being there make it better? Or harder?

"Working with Tom is exercising the art of surrender. He is a fantastic raconteur and really it is my job to listen and admire. The difference now is that he appreciates that, and even, occasionally asks for my opinion in return. I'm actually writing a story for us at the moment. A bit scared because he isn't backward in coming forward on his opinion of a script!!!"

What do you think the role of a companion is?

"The role of the companion is to be there to say 'what is it, Doctor?' so the audience can eavesdrop on the reply. They are also there to depict loyalty, and to flag up moral questions and open debate.

"Occasionally they are there to be brave, or to be rescued, and lately for flirting. I was actually quite shocked with the first kiss in the film, but that could be just me being very old fashioned."

Does the society in which we live alter that?

"Absolutely, I would never be allowed that knife now, for example, and the sex and flirting is very much to do with the times don't you think?"

Leela was a very modern companion, despite being a "savage", she wasn't stupid. How did you find that balance between instinct and intellect?

"I think that was her strength, her instincts and visceral intelligence are what the writers found and still find, the best thing to write about. Never stupid.

Were you conscious, for instance, to instil Leela with the dignity and grace you found in her because of her costume, perhaps, to show she was more than just there for "the dads". Is that something you worked harder at than say, Elisabeth or Mary had to?

"I don't know how Mary or Lis worked. I was never in the room.

"But I would like to say here how very sad it has been over the last two years to lose both these amazing women, and Nick and Carry John and my dear friend Pennant Roberts. It has been a sorrowful time for the 'golden era' - and I knew Mary for forty-four years, from RADA onwards. And I wish with all my heart that she was still here.

"To return to your question... I never performed 'for the dads' and was genuinely surprised when I became known as this 'sex symbol' - Leela was moral, strong, uneducated, a warrior, knew right from wrong, and all that translated into her body language as well as her text and vocal quality.... All of it became the sum of her. A lot of an actor's work is not conscious, it evolves and you end up with a complete and heart felt piece. Technique is necessary, but it is only a tool. All of it goes back to objectives, and bouncing from a place of truth with the energy flowing outwards. Can you guess I teach from time to time?"

Would you like to appear as Leela again in the main tv show?

"Yes but at the age I am now, not stretched and botoxed. I think she would have a football team of children and grandchildren, and be revered as some wise old guru..... But really I'd like to return as a baddy queen... A completely different character, a match for the master, perhaps called the mistress!!!"

Philip Hinchcliffe

Returning to the beginning of Tom's era, I spoke to the man who took over from the stellar Barry Letts. Philip Hinchcliffe was the architect of what has often been referred to as the Golden Age of *Doctor Who*. Speaking to him, I was struck by his sharpness, his intellect, his keenness. I found him friendly in the extreme, but also intense, intimidating, spellbinding. The word 'legend' is bandied around perhaps too often, but, in terms of Tom Baker's unassailable Doctor and, arguably, the most spectacular period in the show's entire fifty year history, Philip Hinchcliffe is just such a legend. I end the Tom Baker era with the man who created it.

How much were you involved in the casting and development of the Fourth Doctor?

"Well, Tom had been cast, but the first one, 'Robot', hadn't been produced. I was appointed round about April and I knew that I would be working with someone already cast. I was just trailing during 'Robot' though, so I had no input, other than the costume, which was done in conjunction with Jim Acheson."

Was the costume a lot of Tom or did he just start dressing like the fourth Doctor?

"Haha, probably. He wasn't one of those men who were very aware of style, but he's a lot smarter now, but it was designed not as a uniform but as clothes. A lot of actors do that, kind of throw things together, aren't they, to find a part. I never really noticed that he dressed like the Doctor outwith the studio. Maybe it was after my time."

He's literally dressed as the Doctor in the pictures from his wedding to Lalla Ward?

"Ah yes, that makes sense. I was on a BFI panel with him a little while ago – he's so funny – and he spoke about finding it much more fun being the Doctor than being Tom Baker, so that makes perfect sense. Life imitating art there, absolutely. Of course, in his mind, there was never any confusion, I think he just loved the persona. He took it very seriously, and had this recognition and adulation he didn't have as just another actor. It really was a role that defined him and he loved living it. When you speak to Tom you're speaking to the Doctor."

Did you feel you had to make your mark on the series? Did you set out to make it different?

"Oh yes very much so. I looked at the programme and spent time analysing it and read quite widely in general science fiction. I felt that I wanted to make it a bit more... plausible? Maybe that's not the right word. Adult? Ah, maybe not...to appear to adults, definitely, more compelling perhaps. So I paid a lot more attention to atmosphere, to design and lighting, and tried to stay away from the old fashioned pantomime villain, which made me a bit upset when in the first season I inherited things like the Cybermen and the Daleks, because that seemed to me to be what younger children liked, and I wanted to explore what we could do with the franchise.

"Barry and Terrance were terrific, but I wanted to change all that, get away from the James Bond, Carnaby Street, you know, all that, because to me I was younger and felt a slightly different zeitgeist, so paid attention to atmosphere and design, and tried to get away from invasion of earth stories which were really rather repetitive. So that was probably the big sort of change and to try and be more sci-fi. We had some stories that were more sci-fi based and also to bring in the alien element in a more imaginative way, so it didn't just have to be an actor in a rubber suit. If you analyse my stories quite a lot of them have the alien or monster element fragmented into various elements in the story, not just a monster. So I worked all that out in the beginning and it gradually evolved with my collaboration with Bob Holmes."

Bob Holmes famously said "let's scare the little buggers," and rewrote 'Genesis of the Daleks' and 'Ark In Space' to appeal more the Philips vision of a darker Doctor Who.

"I think I gave Bob more reign and encouraged him to indulge that. In the stories he wrote for Barry he tried that, and in fact in 'Terror of the Autons' with dolls coming alive etc he did do it, but then, I liked what he was bringing to the series, his scripts had a richness and texture."

Do you think Bob's depth and texture is missing from the new series?

"Yeah it's different. It's a different structure. We had an old fashion serial, which was virtually like live tv. Like the old Saturday morning serials or Radio shows like *Dick Barton*. You had to make an appointment to sit in or you would miss it. Therefore, the serial structure, really, equals the length of a Hollywood movie, so you had to come back.

"Now, they just do mini movies, which, with a story structure like that, makes things move a lot faster. There isn't room for the script to breath or the characters to develop or make more of an impact. It's geared more to a modern audience used to a modern world and storytelling from like video games etc. The storytelling is zappier and faster on the whole, but then, if you look at *really* good drama, like *West Wing, Mad Men, Homeland*, they are given lots of room to breathe and are beautifully written. *Doctor Who* is more action, so you're not going to get that. We were working mostly on the same set, shot in real time, with more dialogue, so it feels like they were longer and more leisurely, which, of course, they were."

How important was the triumvirate of Holmes/Hinchcliffe/Baker?

"Oh absolutely vital. Who knows what it would have been like with another actor? Something happened too when Bob was working with me that brought something new or extra out of him. I don't think my tenure would have been half as successful with another, or run of the mill script editor."

Terrance Dicks famously said he kept a tight reign on Holmes, not allowing him his excesses. Did you let him away with more?

"No, I disagree. I never gave Bob carte blanche. Lots of areas I would stop Bob. You've no idea. Haha. I know Terrance has said I did, but it's not true. He just came up with very, very good ideas that mirrored what I was thinking for the series at the time."

You famously cared more about story, and homage, perhaps, than canon and continuity. Would that be fair?

"Well that was Bob, to be quite honest. I was only twenty-nine when I joined and he was talking about *Curse of the Mummy* and the Five Fingered whatsit, and I'd never seen them. So it was Bob who was consciously doing the homages, not me."

Was continuity important?

"Well that was Bob as well. He never, ever liked, for instance, the pussy footing oriental type of Barry's time. He was into Buddhism and saw them

116

as wise and inscrutable. Bob wanted something else, which is not what I saw, sort of squabbling academics, and the design pushed them further in that way. I think it's more visual than in the script to be honest."

How was Tom to work with?

"Well, by his own admission Tom said he could be a nightmare, but he wasn't during my time. He and I never had a crossed word, and as far as I know he never had a cross word with any director. We had a good, respectful relationship between each other and both wanted what was best for the series. I wouldn't let him change one word of the script, but I'd always do him the courtesy of prepping him for upcoming scripts, making him feel an important part in the creative process, you know, I'd get him excited about stuff – "Tom, we're going to this Italian village..." etc etc so he didn't feel he was just turning up and saying the words, but, on the other hand, we wouldn't put up with any interference. We got on really, really well.

"!He loved Dougie Camfield and David Maloney, he was very fond of the production repertory company under my tenure. It's like when you buy a new car maybe, because I got Tom at the start, I got the best of him, then someone else buys it off you and you start getting problems. Maybe that's what it was! Then he got a bit bored and began to flex his muscles a bit.

"I mean, I don't really know, but I suspect, if there developed a creative vacuum, or if it went in a direction he didn't like, he'd probably gone from being a senior partner to not so much, so wanted to steer a ship he may have felt may have gone off course."

Did you like the change in direction when you left? The new production team (Graham Williams/Douglas Adams) were instructed to tone down the horror, for instance.

"You see, I think that's more a failure of nerves than anything else. And I think it was a misreading of what the true strength, appealing, and drive of the show was. And in some ways it's also very patronising, you know, that some executive is thinking "this show is for children!" is misguided and ultimately put the show heading in the wrong direction. It really went in the wrong direction when John Nathan-Turner came in. I think I'm right in this, because, if you look at the new series, since it's come back, I spoke to Russell T Davies, and discussed it having that imaginative muscularity I tried to instil in it, and, despite it being very different it's still soaked in those ideas and drive."

Obviously Russell T Davies and Steven Moffat were brought up on the Hinchcliffe Era...

"Yeah, Russell said to me, it's only because of you that this can happen, I grew up watching your show."
And of course the Zygons are back!

"Are they really? Oh I didn't know that. Those, of course, were a wonderful creation by Jim Acheson who did a wonderful job. The good thing about those costumes is that you had like a human torso but those funny heads stuck on, which took away the human silhouette, but what Jim did was say, you have to get rid of the neck, and it's marvellously alien. We still had eyes and face and mouth, but if you look at the shape of the spine it's such a different shape. Only thing is, and here's a tip, you must never show their feet! Never shoot any monster from below the ankles. Feet never work. They were a brilliant, brilliant design. The new producers are incredibly clever. Have you seen the new Cybermen? I mean they look like something from Star Wars. The actual design was so updated and wow! So I'm sure the Zygons will be brilliant too!"

So, your episodes story by story?

"'The Ark In Space' – That was my first story going out and it was a complete disaster because we had to rewrite the scripts completely, so I had to not only persuade Bob to write it, but talk the BBC into letting him. I was full of trepidation because, here was I on a brand new job and I didn't have a story to work on. My heart was in my mouth. There was this idea of the spaceship, a design etc, ready, so we had the basics made, and I was really thrilled when Bob came in with a really great script. I learnt lessons there. The cryogenic set was a wonderful job by Roger (Murray Leach). I also learned about lighting, to tone it down, despite the sci-fi setting, and the Wirrn worked much better then. And bubblewrap! No one knew about it then, but it is a bit poor. The power of the story is, well let's face it, it's *Alien*, which came after. It was very dramatic and loved by the public, and it definitely marked a departure. It also got very high ratings, which is great.

"'The Sontaran Experiment' – That was a little two hander, and interesting in the sense that it was all done on location with outdoor, outweight cameras.

"'Genesis of the Daleks' – I was very pleased with that. Terry was a great writer, very much a film writer, so we had to pair it back a bit, but David Maloney understood what I wanted to do with the story and the Daleks. We also had this wonderful character Davros, and the way David shot it, with different angles etc, more excitely, so we don't just have pepperpots going round on a studio floor. David also came up with that shrouded, dark, mysterious start with the Time Lord. Get the lights down, faster, pacy. A great start.

"'Revenge of the Cybermen' – I wasn't so happy with that. Michael Bryant is a fabulous director, as shown on 'Robots of Death', but Bob didn't have a lot of time and I didn't like the aliens. It was filmed at Wookie Hole and whilst there is an aura about the Cybermen, I didn't like it.

"'Terror of the Zygons' – a charming story. Great actors, great Scottish setting. We did brilliantly with the Zygons, but very poorly with the stop motion monster. It's an example of what we cannot do on a shoestring.

"'Planet of Evil' – I liked the idea of *Jekyll and Hyde*. Yeah, I liked that one.

"'Pyramid of Mars' – One of my favourites. It's when I discovered I could merge this sort of futuristic element in a historical period. We created a kind of formula with the historical explained by the science fiction. It was a Bob Holmes rewrite.

"'The Android Invasion' – I liked this kind of sixties' Terry Nation script which worked well in the *Doctor Who* formula. It could have been an Avengers script, but it worked well for us.

"'The Brain of Morbius' – Well Terrance wrote it but didn't like that Bob did a page one rewrite. I have to admit it was a bit more monstrous than I had envisioned! Philip Madoc is fantastic.

"'The Seeds of Doom' – A good idea, I like the two hander in the Arctic, a bit like the movie *The Thing*, and again, what I think we did well, blowing my own trumpet, is that you always remember the setting, we made a stamp on the place, gave each an atmosphere. We managed to create the world of the story. The atmosphere of each was very distinctive.

"'The Masque of Mandragora' - Well that epitomises what I was saying. I'd been to Portmerion, realised the costumes were all in store, so we could do it quite cheaply. It's such a rich setting.

"'The Hand of Fear' – I think the first part works very well, I love the creepy hand etc. Lis and Tom rewrote their goodbye scene. We hadn't paid too much attention to it, so they asked to put something in, which was better than the script.

"'The Deadly Assassin' – Well we had Mary Whitehouse all over us on this one, but you gotta have a cliffhanger. Everyone knows the Doctor isn't going to die. It isn't a show for four or five year olds. She managed to make such a fuss we'd to make an edit, but I still maintain we got it right the first time.

"'The Face of Evil' – This went really well. We had Louise of course. When I first saw her costume I was shocked. I hadn't seen her legs before, and she looked a lot more womanly than I'd thought she would. We had to organise a quick press release too because her appointment was leaked. We blooded a new writer too, so I was very pleased

"'The Robots of Death' – well I wanted to do a robot story, as part of my tenure, and I said why can't we do a murder story, so Bob suggested a certain Agatha Christie novel, and I'd read *Dune*, so we put the three ideas together. Michael Bryant loved the idea, so when over the top with the costumes. It has style, grace and a great story. I saw it recently for the BFI, and it has a brilliant script too. A real classic.

"'The Talons of Weng Chiang' – I loved that. We'd always wanted to do a Victorian, and I said "Why don't you write one!" and he said "No, I'm tired," but I managed to persuade him to do it! We were up against deadlines, but again the BBC does this period very well, so we managed to pull it out of the bag. One of my favourites

Tom Baker would go on to work with another two Producers after Philip Hinchcliffe, and his sticky relationship with Graeme Williams was nothing compared with the relationship he would eventually have with John Nathan-Turner, who himself would go on to be one of the most controversial figures in *Who* history. His first big job though, was to change the Fourth Doctor, and, after seven years of being the Doctor, Tom moved on.

More of JNT soon, but for now, we concentrate on the Fifth Doctor...

The Fifth Doctor Era

Welcome aboard... I'm the Doctor! Or I will be if this regeneration works out!

John Nathan Turner's reign as producer ramped up a gear with the arrival of Peter Davison.

Davison, well known on television already, had huge concerns about taking on the role, but had decided he couldn't really refuse it and, approaching the role with a much more open mind than Tom Baker had latterly shown, his appointment allowed JNT to mould the series into something that was much more his own vision.

The companions got younger, the costumes more staged, the past was alluded to much more and everything, including the Cybermen and Daleks, was given a glitzy eighties make over.

Terry Molloy

One of the enemies to be given a new, slick look, along with a new, slick actor, was the Dalek creator, Davros. Originally played with simmering menace by Michael Wisher, and, perhaps, less successfully by David Gooderson, Terry Molloy became the third incarnation of this maniacal menace, and would remain so throughout the 80s, and, indeed, until Julian Bleach replaced him in the new series.

In this interview, conducted over some time, I chatted to him, not just about his life and experiences as Davros, but about Davros himself, his thought processes, his motivation and his reasoning. It is an insight not just to a veteran actor, eighties *Doctor Who* and Big Finish, but to the most enduring character in Doctor Who's history.

What made you want to become an actor?

"My first career choice was to be a vet, but when I discovered at school that I was totally lacking any ability for science subjects I had to think again. I studied Music and Drama at Liverpool in the mid 60s, but spent most of my time playing sax with a soul band in clubs like The Cavern. It was the era of Northern Soul, just post 'Beatles' – a very vibrant time, and I was tempted to turn pro and become a session musician but as I am a lazy swine I thought that might be too much like hard work, whereas I found acting easier, I enjoyed it a lot more, and discovered that as a 'career choice' it came with more "days off"!

"In fact, my mother had been on the stage from the age of 12, working in

124

Variety during the 20s, 30s and 40s as a juvenile and later as a soubrette with most of the famous names of the day in British Variety and Music Hall - so I suppose performing was in my genes."

How did your early career go?

"Like most actors at that time and probably even more so nowadays it was brief periods of 'work' followed by long periods of 'resting' by which I mean signing on the dole, cleaning flats, grabbing any temp work going etc etc etc! I started out in 1968 by joining a children's theatre company – Theatre Centre – touring all over the UK and performing in schools. In 1969, I found acting work in repertory theatre at the Victoria Theatre in Stoke-on-Trent and then moved to Birmingham to join the Midlands Arts Centre and the Birmingham Rep… from there I began my career in radio."

You joined the Archers in 1973… how did that happen?

"By 1971/2 I had done a few Radio Plays for Antony Cornish, the head of Radio Drama at BBC Pebble Mill in Birmingham and he suggested me to Tony Shryane – the editor of *The Archers* – who was looking for an actor to come into the programme and play a new character, 'Mike Tucker', the herd manager at Brookfield Farm. I did an audition and was offered the part for what, I was told, was to be just 5 weeks… 37 years later and "Moike" is still here – now the curmudgeonly Ambridge milkman!"

How has it changed over the years? And how has your character developed?

"*The Archers* started out in 1951 as a drama based farming information programme and over the years has morphed into a highly successful radio

125

soap that is coming close to it's sixtieth birthday, with over five million listeners. But for me, I think *The Archers* has always been a little pool of sanity in an otherwise insane world and the reason it has survived so long has been not only due to the hard work of the production team and their advisors in always accurately reflecting the reality of living in a rural community, but their foresight in meticulously nurturing younger generations in the story lines to carry the programme forward. All this driven by the superbly drawn characters portrayed with real truth and conviction of the 60 strong team of actors on the programme.

"'Mike Tucker' started out as the herd manager of Brookfield Farm and after thirty-six years of trials and tribulations is beginning to find his equilibrium. But he rarely opens his mouth except to change feet and, as an honest son of the soil, suffers fools with no gladness whatsoever! Also, like Davros, he now only has one eye!

"It has a following as enthusiastic as *Doctor Who* doesn't it?"

Which are you known for more?

"I am know equally well in both camps for both characters, the joy of which is that as in neither do you get to see my face I am able to move freely and anonymously about the world without any of those dreaded "Oi! Didn't you used to be....?" moments!"

How did you end up with the part of Davros in 'Resurrection'?

"Thanks to the director Matthew Robinson, whom I had previously been working with on another TV series *Radio Phoenix*, about a commercial radio station, where I had been playing a sort of 'Smashy & Nicey' DJ character. When Matthew first asked me to play Davros, I had little idea of who the character was. Yes, I knew of the Daleks as I had watched *Doctor Who* in the early Hartnell and Troughton days, but after that 'I got a life' as an old girlfriend once rather archly put it! Matthew sat me down an showed me 'Genesis' and then said, "Do you think you could re-create that character?". For some strange reason I found myself saying, 'Yes'!"

How did you approach the part? Did you watch Michael Wisher and David Gooderson?

"To bring Davros back in 'Resurrection' it was most important to have Michael Wisher's creation of the character as a reference and starting point. It was never the intention to do a carbon copy of Michael's performance – that would have been mere caricature – and the truth of the character lost in the process. My aim was to re-create the essence of Davros to the best of my ability retaining those essential elements of the original conception and then building on that as the script demanded.

"My research was based on viewing the tapes of 'Genesis' and 'Destiny', then working out how Michael Wisher and David Gooderson had produced the 'voice' of Davros, as I felt this held one of the keys to the character along with the degree of disability that was displayed by the restriction of the character's movement – a lot of which was informed and driven by the physical restrictions of the mask and the chariot. The actual intention, direction and drive of Davros as a character leapt off the page at me from Eric Saward's 'excellent' script (forgive the Davrosism there!)."

You (thankfully!) got a new mask for your portrayal. How important are the prosthetics in getting into character?

"When I took on the role, the decision was made to create a new mask using my head as a template, so a head cast was made and from that Stan Mitchell modelled the new face of Davros. Because the foam latex used was quite firm and unforgiving, the result was that I needed to speak with an over exaggerated movement of the face and jaw in order to produce any sort of external movement in the mask. This then informed and partly dictated the delivery of the speeches and was instrumental in how Davros' voice was eventually formed. And in my view about 90% of the character is contained in that voice!"

You brought, I think, a pomposity to Davros – do you see him as a snob?

"Not a snob, but with that certainty of status and an inherited haughtiness that can be the mark of certain patrician families… and definitely within Davros' family. You'll have to listen to the Big Finish mini-series "I, Davros" to see that was just a starting point for our story of Davros' journey from boy to 'monster'. His obsession with science and lack of ability to socialise with those he considers of lesser intellect than himself, point to a darker root within."

Do you have sympathy for him? IS he an evil genius, or just one whose life run away from him?

"Now that's a philosophical can of worms…! Let me chuck a few questions back! What do you consider to be the definition of genuine evil – and who can, or on what basis should it be defined? Do you believe that 'evil' is the result of nature or nurture or a combination of the two – is a newborn baby evil at birth or does it assimilate 'evil' ways as he/she grows? Take 'Revelation' as an example. Davros solves the problem of hunger and starvation throughout the galaxy saving billions of lives in the process – Is this an heroic act worthy of universal acclaim and praise, or a deeply evil and shameful act because he used the bodies of people who

128

were already dead to create the protein to feed the starving of the universe? You decide... and that decision must and will be informed by the particular moral or ethical standpoint you hold. I don't posit a preference either way, except to say that I find it more interesting to play a character that has shades of both light and dark in their persona, the grading of those shades is then how the character is ultimately perceived."

He once described the Doctor as "the closest thing he has to a friend" How true is this do you think?

"Absolutely true! I think both the Doctor and Davros have come to realise that as well as being on a totally equal intellectual footing, they are also both ultimately... alone! Those are strong bonds that tie them together and which, under different circumstances, could have led to friendship."

In 'Resurrection' he is brought back from cryogenic freezing... was he aware during that time? Did the process affect him?

"I can't remember where it was that Davros describes the feeling of mentally going back over his entire life in the minutest painful detail and that long painful mental process filling just one second of his imprisonment before starting all over again like a loop continuing into infinity... you tell me if it affected him?"

How did you want to evolve the character during 'Revelation'? There is a marked sense of humour, which comes across perhaps for the first time...

"Indeed, there was a desire and intention to begin to move slightly away from the 'Intergalactic Reich' of 'Genesis' and begin to explore other facets of a character that otherwise could have become just a two dimensional caricature 'monster' — hence the injection of a black humour to some of his lines."

By now of course Davros is setting up his own "escape routes" whereas before it seemed down mainly to luck… do you think he really always expects the Doctor to appear and scupper his plans?

"His escape routes are contractual! Terry Nation insisted that Davros (although possibly appearing to be doomed or even destroyed) always had an escape pod, route, or whatever at his disposal. Like any good chess player Davros would have thought through all possible scenarios before facing his greatest opponent."

How was it being just a head for most of 'Revelation of the Daleks'… uncomfortable?

"About as uncomfortable as you can imagine, being sealed in a hot foam latex mask and then bolted into a revolving Perspex cylinder with your legs tied up under the swivel chair you are sitting on to facilitate your spinning round and not 'kneecapping' yourself on the steel uprights of the set!"

And then of course you actually do *become a head! Or do you? I know that BF audios suggest this is the case (after the bomb goes off in Davros' chair), but later* Who *episodes ('Journey's End') show a Davros very much the man he was…*

What did you think of the story 'Remembrance of the Daleks'… it sidelines Davros quite a bit.

"'Remembrance' was slated for production at a time when I was contracted to and working on a TV drama series for Central called *Tales of Sherwood Forest* (In fact *nothing* to do with Robin Hood - it was set in a

130

Nottingham wine bar!!) so I almost was not in 'Remembrance' but for the good offices of both Producers who sat down and worked out a schedule that would fit both of their needs ending with me basically dashing into Television Centre record on one day between location filming days in Nottingham. I don't know about sidelined.. I was certainly breathless!"

'Terra Firma' suggests that Davros has an identity crisis, the irony of wanting to be the leader and creator but realizing he can only do that by becoming a Dalek... the Emperor... how do you think he got out of that one (and obviously when the Emperor is seen next in 'A Parting of the Ways' he isn't Davros...)

"A great story, and such a delight to play that degeneration into complete schizophrenia. Obviously he doesn't become either a Dalek or The Emperor it is all in his head as part of the mind games he and the Doctor almost relish playing with each other!"

You've worked with Doctors Davison, Baker, McCoy and McGann... each with a different persona, which Davros seems to relish in "getting to know". Do you as an actor change how Davros is to accommodate the actor opposite, or do you think Davros does?

"Er….. No, and… er…. No!"

Would it be fair to suggest he has an affinity for Colin's Doctor…? They almost get on…

"No more or less than any other Doctor… it's just that you have heard and seen Davros more with Colin's Doctor than with any of the others. It is true that Colin and I have a lot of fun working together and that might give an extra frisson to some of the things we have recorded, but I think you have to look at this question in the light of the answer I gave to an

131

earlier question about the Doctor and Davros' "friendship" - the answer lies there."

I presume you've watched Davros's return in 'The Stolen Earth'... where you disappointed not to be able to resurrect someone who's been part of your life for such a long time?

"I didn't watch the episode when it went out as I was about 600 miles from the North Pole in Svalbard at the time, and I didn't actually see the episode until a few months ago by chance while watching TV in a hotel I was staying at. I think I can certainly say that I was deeply disappointed not to be offered the chance of bringing the character into the new series – but ultimately, that decision was not in my hands."

What did you think of that whippersnapper Bleach?

"Probably along the same lines as Michael Wisher thought about me when I took over the role from him!"

Do you like the new series in general? Choice of Doctors etc?

"Overall I think they have done a splendid job in linking the past (or Classic Series as it is now called) with the New Series. My favourite episodes over the four series have been 'Dalek', 'The Empty Child' & 'The Doctor Dances', 'The Girl in the Fireplace', 'Blink' and 'Silence in the Library' – they have all contained that dark quality and depth of narrative texture in the writing that is so vital to a really good *Doctor Who* story. The Doctors have been superb, especially David Tennant, though I do think it is time for an older Doctor once more, and as for the Master? Derek Jacobi was the chillingly obvious choice! Why the change?

132

And of course you did Scarifyers, *with Nicholas Courtney – how did that come about, and what do you think of it?*

"I was simply sent the script by Simon Bernard who asked if I would be interested in playing the role of Professor Edward Dunning (elderly ghost story writer) opposite Nick Courtney as Detective Superintendant Lionheart (octogenarian ex-copper). I read and loved the 'tongue in cheek' writing style (set in the 1930s, a sort of mix of *Dick Barton Special Agent* and *The X Files*) and blatant comedy of the first script and immediately said yes!

"At the time of writing this there have now been five installments as we have just released episode four - 'The Curse of the Black Comet' - with Brian Blessed guesting as the totally inept explorer and tomb raider 'Sir Basil Champion'. And with episode five – "The Secret Weapon of Doom" – just recorded, with Leslie Phillips and Nigel Havers as guest stars, I think *The Scarifyers* is going from strength to strength. Nick and I had never worked together before this, but it is a partnership I truly enjoy as our two old characters resonate so beautifully together in their own idiosyncratic ways."

Back to the oldest son of Skaro - would you don the mask and hand again?

"If you look closely at my forehead you will see they're tattooed in letters of fire – 'Never Again!'"

Do you have a message for all Skarosians out there?

"Tar lubeck Ka'Leed – uth ricta Dal'ek"

If you don't know what it means, listen to "I, Davros" and all will be made clear… a rough translation from the ancient 'Dal' prophetic script (the original language of Skaro) would be...

"And so the Men (Ka'Leed) – shall become Gods (Dal'ek)"

Think on that…..!!!!

Mark Strickson

As companions go, perhaps more than in any other era, JNT went for "broad strokes" and "types" as opposed to characters. Maybe the one exception to that would be the character of Vizlor Turlough, someone initially designed for one purpose only – destroy the Doctor.

I chatted to the nicest man in Who-dom (well, another nicest man) Mark Strickson about his time on Who, Turlough and, well, whale sharks. You probably don't want to know...

"I look like shit!" says Mark. "But this is as good as it gets, I'm afraid! Can we keep the webcam off?"

We then discuss the weather in New Zealand and how Scottish it is. "We're more Scottish than you, we wake up to the sound of bagpipes. Scots love it! It's fu*%in' horrible!!!" Various Scottish accents abound, along with far too many swear words!

Should we discuss Doctor Who at some point?

"Not sure what I'll remember to be honest, but crack on!"

Did you realise you'd be talking about Who 30 years on?

"JNT warned me that I'd suddenly become a name, but, to be honest, I didn't. I mean, I did when I got on telly, but that took three or four months. I'd been on *Angels* beforehand so knew the score a bit, so I'd keep my job as a barman in London, cos I lived in a little council flat near the Old Vic. People thought that was funny, but as an actor, don't give up the day job! But in some sense JNT was right, but, wait, is it only thirty years??? When I first joined, I had to go to America a lot... there was a bus going around, for some reason, publicising the series, and we were asked to go. Made to go really because it was the BBC's most profitable franchise. So we started going back and forward to America and realised when thousands of people showed up so I began to think, yeah, this is huge."

And Longleat took you by surprise too?

"Oh yes, it was massive. I'm living in this council flat in Waterloo and the BBC say we'll send a chauffeur driven car to take you, and I said 'Whatever you do, don't send it to the flat!' because usually on a Saturday morning when you woke up there'd be a few doors kicked in, a bit of trouble, it was pretty violent, and I thought if the BBC send a chauffeur driven car in, I know I'm going to get back and me door will be kicked off or hanging from its hinges, they'll think I'm loaded. So it stopped up the road and I walked. Then trying to get to Longleat, well, that was ridiculous. We couldn't get anywhere near it! They hadn't been expecting all these people, and the roads were all blocked. When we did eventually get there, the Royal Marines were there! I mean, madness, the Royal Marines escorting us around. Absolute madness!"

Turlough's a different type of companion isn't he? How did you approach him?

"Well, it's very difficult when you're brought into a series about what to do. I spoke to John, and I spoke to Eric Saward, and I went out and bought a costume. I was allowed a lot of input into that sort of thing. Turlough's an intelligent character, he's had his own spaceship, he's got his own life, and that was very different from say the girls – I mean, sure they went out to buy dresses, but we were searching for a character when I went out, not just fashion, and we came back with these... well, I thought, it's a public school, but I don't want blazers or anything, so I had a plain black suit. JNT went 'God, you look like a funeral director!' and I said 'Yep, that'll do'. See, funeral directors, they're there at a crucial time in your life, they're really nice to you, but, in the end, they're going to put you under the ground. There's something you don't quite trust about them. So John thought it was too boring, with no colour, so we agreed John could chose the socks, so you'll see, in Mawdryn Undead, there's a shot of me changing gear and I've got on these loud socks, I think they're purple and white, and that's JNT's fault! The rest is mine!"

You're with Whovian royalty in Mawdryn Undead too, aren't you, with Nicholas Courtney?

"Oh that was great, because it made my episode even more memorable for the fans. I mean the fans say I'm one of the most memorable characters, but that's mostly to do with the fact that in my debut I'm trying to kill the Doctor and the Brigadier is there! For the fans, that's huge. And lovely for me because Nick was such a lovely guy, and really supportive. Lovely man with his feet on the ground."

I asked if Mark was aware of the temporal contradictions with Mawdryn?

"Remind me..." So I did... "Ah right, the Blinovitch Effect!"

That's the chap. But the Brig seems to have retired before he joined UNIT.

"I've always said that they should give the scripts out to you guys before they film them, you know way more than us. At conventions I always say 'look, I'm going to answer as best I can but you already know the answer, and better than I do!"

137

You seemed to have a really good time with Peter on the extras of that DVD. Is he as good to work with as he seems?

"Oh yes, he's wonderful, and a good friend. Pete's great. And we were all so young. The reason I had to get my hair cut and coloured so severely at the time is that I looked a bit like Peter, particularly in long shot, with that floppy blonde thing going on, and we were of a similar age, he's only a couple of years older than me, but he looked older and I looked younger. I suppose at 50 it's now a good thing. I'm 53, I was born on April the 6th 1959. I think Wiki get it wrong."

We then have a long conversation about how old we both feel.

"I was confused as my son's granddad the other day. I went, 'watch it mate, you're digging a hole here!'"

Do you think the initial motive for Turlough – to kill the Doctor – was a hindrance to the character?

"Well for the first eight episodes I was the baddie. I think it was good though, because it allowed the writers to bring in a very strong character, with his own plans, his own brain etc. But the problem arises when we want to keep him in the TARDIS, because it makes both him and the Doctor look stupid, so he has to make friends with the Doctor, so essentially he's pretty much like the Doctor, and you can't have him running around, asking questions and getting locked up all the time. Sometimes you can, with the nature of the show, but not all the time."

Was it frustrating when that happened? For example, in 'The Five Doctors' or 'Terminus'?

"It is frustrating, but you know why the script writers do it, because it's not *The Turlough Show*, it's *Doctor Who*. People ask me would I like to go back, and I said I'd love to – to play the Doctor! It's the best part! Or the villain. The villain is great too."

There's a correlation with Turlough and Jack Harkness don't you think?

"Oh yeah... I see what you mean..."

It seems the writers of the new series managed to find an angle for the slightly untrustworthy wideboy Jack where as back in your day perhaps they couldn't...?

"Well it's a different beast now, isn't it? We were aiming for twenty-five minutes on a Tuesday night, and didn't have the resources, really, to push a character like that. That's why the costumes worked. You knew it was Turlough, everytime, you knew it was Tegan, or Nyssa. It's a shorthand. That's why we didn't change the costumes. That's the Doctor, that's the villain, that's the heroine, that's Turlough, and the format could just about cope with that. You couldn't develop Turlough as a character."

Big Finish has managed to help with that though?

"That's great fun. I'm always in England around Christmas, and it's great because we all get together and have some great scripts. I've even done them from abroad, on my own. I got DVT but couldn't travel."

Do you think Turlough would work now? Was he Doctor specific?

"Oh no he'd definitely work now, I'd love to take Turlough back to *Doctor Who*, I think he'd be great, as an older character. Let the fans discover all about him. I'm doing stuff for the fiftieth, but can't say anything about it right now, sorry."

So we went on to discuss his stories individually...

"'Mawdryn Undead' – Mawdryn was great, I loved it. I don't know if people understand how we make television, or at least how you made it in those days but we were on very low budget, so we read the script, did the filming first, then the video... so my first day on *Doctor Who* was filming with the vintage car and the production manager said to me "take the car for a ride, you need to be able to drive it, away you go, see you in a bit"... and I thought, driving this car around beautiful country lanes was "well, you don't get much better jobs that this!" Then I came back and did my first scene, and that was as I walked towards the car and wander around it, get in it with Hippo and drive off. So, obviously, you do it in bits, and the nice thing about it was that JNT was on set and after it he calls me over and goes "Very good, yes, but, well, could you do it in a posher accent?" I said "John, no, no way, I've given you posh and that's as posh as I get" and we had a laugh and he said "You know what, it's fine. You've come from another planet, pretending to be a public schoolboy, that's how we'll go with that!" So that was interesting. And from that point it was lovely, and the guy who played Hippo was a genuinely funny guy and he had me falling around laughing. And the lunch was good... we had wine, in those days, it's spring water now. We'd have to give Nick a nap though, which was fine.

"'Terminus' – well that was Sarah's story, and that's fine, that was good. And as I said we were fighting against the half hour format and Nyssa was one of those characters that everyone likes, and again, I think, because she had a brain, (we talk about Jonathan Morris's 'Prisoners of Fate' for a bit). I thought 'Terminus' was very nicely shot. Obviously Janet and I spent a lot of time crawling around in tunnels and pipes. Now, I had two suits as Turlough when I was in *Doctor Who*, and after 'Terminus' I had to have another one made. I had one for stunt work because I agreed to do most of my own stunts, and one for being all posh in the TARDIS. I actually wore through the stunt suit knees on 'Terminus' with all the crawling around we did. It might say something about the quality of the suit I was wearing, budgets were low. Or the quality of the set! Terminus was fine for me. We just got on with it, it was Sarah's story.

"'Enlightenment' – Yeah this was very much a Tegan and Turlough story and it was fun. I loved working with Lynda Baron, who was an absolute icon of eighties television, so it was great to see her for real. Most memorable. Her daughter worked as a secretary for JNT too. There was two stories going on with 'Enlightenment', and I was a bit confused as to what was going on. Now, Barbara Clegg was the writer, and she, Peter and I did a commentary on the reissue of this story, and the graphics on that cost more than the full story the first time round. But Peter said to her "Barbara, what exactly WAS Enlightenment...? I mean, we chased it and never found out!" And Barbara blustered and said "Well, we were on these ships, and they were racing and...and..." and Peter said "Yes, but what was it...?" Maybe we'll never find out! Maybe that's the point! But Janet was great in this story, she had this weird relationship with this weird guy though. Oh, and here's a story I think you might know. When I through myself into space, I was wearing a harness and crutch thing, and you swing out into space and I through myself off the ship and it broke! It was like hitting a brick wall with my legs apart. You can imagine the pain. I couldn't walk! These days you'd probably sue someone. I just hobbled away. Testicles the size of beach balls, all purple and bruised. And in scenes in the TARDIS you'll see I don't move very much, and that's because I've walloped myself off a brick wall! I couldn't move.

"'The King's Demons' – Ah, Kamelion! Now, I had a lot to do with Kamelion, but the problem with him was very simply – the budget was too low. If you went back a few years to *Star Wars* they were trying all sorts of stuff – simple stuff, a turning head movement and not much else, with some flashing lights, and sort of that's what they wanted with Kamelion. That was the idea, but the fatal error was that they had decided that they were going to have a tape with his dialogue on and he would sync with that. Surely those could just have been laid on afterwards, but they decided not to do that, so we were working with an actor who had strict timings on his dialogue, so we had to fit ours in between. So we'd either be rushing our lines or going... really... slowllllly... to try and fill the gap. And the other issue with him is that even as a robot he didn't work very well. We'd go to the next Kamelion scene and there'd be Kamelion bits lying all over the floor, they hadn't managed to get him together and working probably, and time was a big issue in studios then, so he became an enormous problem in trying to finish on time. He sort of worked, sometimes, he was a good idea, if a little lacking in money. The Daleks, for instance, worked as live, with guys in a little booth who could get the timing right. It's the proper way to do it.

"'The Five Doctors' – Well this was something special. It was nice because we were working with people we'd met at conventions. I'd left *Doctor Who* by then [sic] so my wife at the time and I used to go little drives. One time we did this, around the beautiful Welsh country side, and there was a problem with the film, a scratch or something, and this was before mobile phones, so no one could get a hold on me. It was on local radio etc, but we didn't have a radio in this little VW Beetle. We got as far as Stratford on Avon and someone went "Mark, Mark, Mark! You have to go back!"

"There's an interesting story on acting styles from this. Obviously *Doctor Who* isn't real life, it's a fantasy, and requires a certain style, a heightened response, to a monster or something. It's much more difficult to make that seem real, from say like normal acting, because in that you respond to what someone is saying to you. There's an emotion. In *Doctor Who*, short scenes, instant emotion, no time to get there. "In this scene, Mark, you're being sucked out into space and scream! Go!" Now that is not easy acting, and by the time we got to 'The Five Doctors' Peter and I had been doing other things, and had become very low key. We did this scene together and JNT came over and said "That's all very good, but you're back on *Doctor Who* now, can you ACT?"

"'Warriors of the Deep' – Oh this is a classic case of that. The Myrka! We had to react against this bloody thing from *Rentaghost*! This was a big issue. A classic case in point. The Myrka is chasing you and can't move a leg, so we have to believe it's coming at us. (Is it hard not to laugh?) No, not at all, because we have to find a honesty, an integrity, and really believe, because, if you don't, you're going to look shit in *Doctor Who*. It's got to be real. It must be. You'll find the regulars in all the eras will see that. You have to believe. If you watch *Spider-Man*, you want to believe it, so the guy who's playing him has to believe it. Same goes for *Doctor Who*.

"'The Awakening' – Yeah it was an interesting little story. I didn't remember much about it because it was so quick. I remember going out for a drive one day, and we stopped at this little village for a drink and a sandwich and I'm thinking "I've been here before…" then I realised why! I went back with Nick Briggs too. More drinks.

"'Frontios' – Oh that was quite good, a strong one for me. Although again, instant emotion required screaming "Tractators, Tractators,

Tractators!" which is where the example came from. Interestingly with that, John was in the studio again and he said "Mark, that was very good, but please don't spit on the cameras!" Apparently Leonard Rossiter was terrible for that. I understand Timothy Dalton, David Tennant etc were spitting quite a bit in David's finale too. I didn't see it but do try to watch a lot of *Doctor Who* when I can. In fact, being in New Zealand I got a phone call telling me Colin Baker was on *I'm A Celebrity*, but I missed it as I was in Africa. I'm away from televisions a lot. I mean, there's me, lying on the floor in a jungle in Africa trying not to get shot at and Colin's on *I'm a Celebrity*. He wants to try MY life! Haha.

"'Resurrection of the Daleks' – This is actually my favourite episode. I loved working with the Daleks, they're iconic, they're the first thing you think about when you think about *Doctor Who* and it's very political. Eric's stories can divide viewers, of course, but, like you, I'm in the love camp. You only need to have 50% of people loving it for it to be a success. Like *Shameless*. Or *Big Brother*. 50% of people would never ever watch it, but as long as 50% switch on its brilliant.

"'Planet of Fire' – I decided to leave. In retrospect I wish I hadn't, I should have stayed. I don't regret leaving, as it took me into new parts of my life, and that's not a bad thing. I've had ups and downs but that was an up, and it was a wonderful time. Peter was lovely, Janet was lovely, Sarah was lovely, JNT was lovely. Turlough and the sixth Doctor would have worked quite well I think, but when I decided to leave I didn't know Colin and Nicola was coming in or I would have stayed. But there you are, it wasn't to be. I'd made my decision and I stuck to it."

A final question – was JNT good or bad for Doctor Who?

"He was undoubtedly good for it. Brilliant for it. He understood what it

144

needed. When he came it, it was an ailing franchise and it needed a kick up the arse. He gave it that kick up the arse, and personally got on the road and sold it, weekend after weekend. I know John loved that, but it's good to love your job. Never forget he was working, this was a job. I think some people think this was some sort of perk but all I can say is that my idea of hell is to get on a plane for a weekend and come back and do my day job. Until you've got off a plane and worked your bollocks off you don't know. That's hard work. My run is particularly quality, with writing, acting... we worked very hard as a team and got the best product out we could on the budget we had."

The Sixth Doctor Era

Change, my dear, and it seems not a moment too soon...

As one of the most popular tenures, in terms of viewing figures, ended and Peter Davison left the series, the new Doctor was garish, grumpy and, initially unpopular. But nobody could have guessed that the show was about to enter its most tumultuous period ever.

I spoke about the approach to the writing, with Philip Martin, what it's like to be a villain with Nabil Shaban, how a companion works with Nicola Bryant and, of course, being the Doctor, with none other than Colin Baker.

Philip Martin

Philip Martin is a classic series *Who* writer with an impeccable set of credentials. Not only a stalwart, as an actor and writer, of BBC classics like *Z Cars* and creator of the gritty, controversial drama *Gangsters*, he also created the iconic *Doctor Who* villain - are you reading this Steven? - Sil.

I sat down with Philip for tales of Varos, marsh minnows and PJ Hammond...

What made you want to be a writer?

"I was a professional actor who evolved into a writer. As to why? I felt I had stories I had to tell and an almost obsessive desire to bring them into the world."

For many aspiring writers, the leap from writing to professional writing is a huge one. How did you manage it, other than, of course, talent? (Was Z Cars your first commission?)

"Yes, getting that first writing credit is vital, you're right. Z Cars was my first TV credit. I'd acted in a number of episodes, so knew the show. But any aspiring writer can gain that same advantage by really studying a programme or a genre they wish to write for. I've given a series of interviews that I hope will help new writers to avoid common pitfalls – the interviews, together with free writing tips, can be found on www.howtowritesuccessfully.com"

Something I've always wanted to know – what's the 'everyday' like for a professional writer – disciplined? Free? Boring? Exciting?

"All of these, but professional writers have to find a way to write no matter what is going on around them. Also he/she is always turning ideas or current story problems over in their mind. Again, there is much more about the differing aspects of the writing life on my website."

You worked on established series such as Shoestring and Gangsters, even though you created that. Is this a more difficult discipline than writing 'from new', as it were. Do constraints help or hinder?

"Firstly, *Gangsters* doesn't qualify – the whole shebang was mine, from the original movie to the 12-part series that followed. Writing for established series has its own special demands. It's great to have freedom, but curiously, to tell your story within series constraints can create a real buzz when you pull it off. Writing for *Z Cars* as my first TV credit was a baptism of fire – not only writing for a popular top ten show but with a police advisor from hell, a stickler for accurate police procedure. It was a tough apprenticeship – I've always been grateful for the help I received from an excellent script editor, PJ Hammond, who guided me through the rapids of popular TV scriptwriting."

And then you got Doctor Who. How did that come about?

"My daughter, Hilary, who must have been eight or nine years old, started to watch *Doctor Who* and was a bit scared. She asked me to watch it with her. Peter Davison was the Doctor. I'd drifted away from the programme but enjoyed viewing it once again. Then, after a couple of weeks, I woke up one morning asking myself, 'What will the media be like in, say, 300 years' time?' That thought led me to muse about a prison planet, with an officer class who kept the population entertained with cruel interactive games of life and death. I sent the idea to Eric Saward, who liked the idea, although John Nathan-Turner was highly suspicious of my motives – he thought I was trying to pedal a political point of view. God knows why. Anyway, I eventually convinced him otherwise and Vengeance on Varos began its eventful journey."

Yes, I was going to ask about 'Varos' and Eric Saward's involvement in it.

"Eric was very important in calming JNT's fears that I was about to turn his baby into a *Play for Today*. At one of our early meetings Eric said something about writing for the show and specifically about setting stories in the distant future. 'You have to create that world, its history, its politics, its people, its climate – everything about it. You must become godlike in your creation', And that was the key to my creating the detail of the harsh world of Varos and its mineral resources, including Zeiton 7. (Remember that?)[Yep, that was the substance needed to make the TARDIS function properly, found only on Varos... - Ed]"

Were you a fan of the series? A favourite Doctor, etc? What did you think of Colin?

As I say, I was a lapsed fan who came back and enjoyed Peter Davison as the Doctor – in fact, the first drafts of 'Varos' were written for him but then he regenerated into Colin. Because we were both new to the show, I watched Colin evolve into 'my Doctor'. I enjoyed writing his lead role, I found I could play off his merrily detached persona with, I believe, some profit for us both.

Creating a memorable character such as Sil - is the character in the writing, the acting, both?

"Definitely both. I wanted a creature who needed water, an amphibian, then Sil took over as all the best characters do, and I realised he was not only a rabid capitalist but an amoral turncoat who was loyal only to himself. This amused me and still does. Nabil was a huge bonus and made the character his own, the irony being that Sil's character is so very different to that of Nabil."

Were you happy with the finished product?

"If you mean Nabil's performance, yes, very. For the 'Varos' story, yes, given the time constraints and the budget limitations, I was satisfied.

Coming back for a second year you wrote 'Mindwarp'. This was notoriously a troubled production. What are your memories of it?

"Mixed. I was pleased to be one of the four writers asked to write the series. I was given episodes five-eight inclusive. Robert Holmes was to write the first four episodes but then things began to go downhill. Bob Holmes became seriously ill and later died. A great writer and a huge loss.

"Then there were troubles with the stories that were to follow mine, there seemed to be a whole raft of conflicting ideas – a writer friend of mine was approached. I asked him what was his idea. 'Daffodils on the moon', I was told. After which I gave up and concentrated on my own section of the Trial and the story of 'Mindwarp', leaving the serial strands and foreshadowing elements for Eric to weave in once the surrounding stories were finally decided upon.

It's considered a confusing story. Was it written like that? How much of it was out of your hands?

"For the reasons given above, I'd estimate only 80% of the produced script was mine. When I was writing I didn't know what was in the episodes before or after; no wonder there's an air of confusion about the whole series. It seemed, from my perspective, rather chaotic."

Eric and John weren't getting on at this point, did that make things harder?

"Well, it didn't help."

What did you think of the finished product?

"I was a little disappointed. I thought the director allowed too many of the cast to spoof it up. I was also annoyed when I later learned that Colin asked for guidance about why he was doing evil things as the Doctor (result of an interrupted brain transfer experiment). Nobody could apparently help and it was said that I was unavailable to explain the reason for his character's behaviour, which was untrue – they just couldn't be bothered to contact me. But there were things about 'Mindwarp'. I liked, Sil, of course, and the transfer of Lord Kiv into Peri's metabolism was, for me, a truly chilling moment."

And of course 'Mindwarp' was a replacement for another story when you'd originally been asked to bring Sil back for 'Mission to Magnus', which contains elements like Kiv and Thoros Beta which echo in 'Mindwarp'. What was the thinking about that?

Sil was proving very popular and JNT had all sorts of plans for merchandising, such as green sweets to be called Marsh Minnows after the delicacies Sil would sometimes swallow. I also wanted to explore the idea of a world dominated by women. What would it mean? How would they rule? Would they be 'deadlier than the male'? How would their world and society be? What would they do if they were threatened? JNT and Eric liked the premise so 'Mission' was commissioned."

Were you 'given' the Ice Warriors or were they your idea?

"It was suggested that it might be a time to introduce an old enemy and the Ice Warriors seemed a good idea at the time, so I said okay."

Did you research them?

"Yes, and to my dismay, when I watched 'The Monster of Peladon' I realised I'd forgotten how very slo-oo-w and cumbersome they were. As I like to move things along in my writing, this was a heart-sinking moment, but later I thought, suppose the temperate world of Magnus could be turned into one of sub-zero temperatures? That would allow the Ice Warriors to come up to speed. This was the breakthrough – all I had to do then was to find a way to alter the axis of the planet. A knowledgeable academic friend suggested a way of achieving this and we were off and running (or lumbering, in the Ice Warriors' case)."

When did you know this serial wouldn't be filmed? This must have been bitterly disappointing.

"I'd completed the script to everyone's satisfaction and was waiting for the production to be scheduled for recording. Often there was a gap before I heard about dates, so I thought the delay was nothing untoward, little knowing what was going on behind the scenes. Yes, of course I was disappointed. I eased some of my frustrations by novelising the script and seeing it published."

How come you didn't write again for the original series?

"Eric had left. JNT had taken over the story direction more or less completely. The series had become too juvenile for my taste and after the hiatus I had moved on to other things such as *Star Cops*."

How did the Big Finish revival happen?

"A phone call to me from David Richardson. I said 'Yes', I'd have a go. Later there was a shock in store when I realised how visual the script was, but I've written award-winning radio drama so I relished the challenge of translating the TV images into audio pictures."

Was the audio version much changed from the original script?

"Only where necessary to fulfil the demands of the sound medium. I wanted to stay as close as possible to my original version."

What did you think of the final version?

"Pleased. And interested in how my younger self had tackled the piece originally given the way the attitudes of society were at the time. I was far from being anti-women both then and now. After the recent release of 'Mission to Magnus' I sense that there is some unease about the strong way the verbal interchanges happen between the sexes in my script. I know the world has changed but I'm damned if I'm going to censor the work of my younger self just to satisfy the po-faced political correctionists who seem blind to humour and the use of irony. Ansor is a Victorian bully with a brutal mind-set, hence his harsh attitude to women."

Are you glad it's out now?

"I'm delighted. After lying doggo in my archive for some twenty-four years, I'm so pleased it's come to life again."

I can't go without asking you: what do you think of the new series? Have you watched it? Do you like Russell's work etc? And what do you think of the choice of Doctors?

"I enjoy the *Doctor Who* of today. My only criticism of the recent series is that it seems to feature aliens invading earth a little too often. I have great respect for Russell T – he's a lifelong fan who brought his reputation, enthusiasm and talent to the revival and made the show the success it is. We owe him an immense vote of thanks. About the Doctors – yes, having leading actors bring their charisma to the role gives it a further ratings boost. Interesting with the latest manifestation, Matt Smith, being so young – it should appeal to a younger generation but not at the expense of the older fan. Russell's achievement was to balance the appeal of the stories between young and older viewers. I hope that is kept in mind by the new production team."

Would you like to write for it?

"Yes, I'd love to give Sil his head in a new story."

Nabil Shaban

And talking of Sil...

Nabil Shaban is an artisan in the true sense of the word. Poet, actor, artist, director and writer, he's a driving force in the rights for actors with disabilities and acting as a whole and is outspoken, opinioned, wise, talented and generous. Taking time out from his many projects, not least of all his latest film, he and I gobbled down some grubs and gurgled away about the return of Sil, the War on Terror and someone called Steven Moffat... whoever HE is!

What made you want to be an actor? What was the journey you took to get there?

"Ever since I was a young child I wanted to be actor, because I wanted to live a fantasy life, I wanted to dress up and experience other realities which were not accessible to me, try out characters and scenarios in a safe environment. For me acting is a temporary moment of madness. An actor is privileged because he or she is licenced to be deluded, to imagine and behave as someone else. I like acting because it's a form of escapism. Also, I love telling stories, and acting is part of the story-making process. However, as I've got older, I've started to question my motives because I've seen that I'm very choosy about what I do, and I've found I don't like all the "Luvvie" elements of the profession…the curtain calls, the applause, the attention, being treated like you are some kind of God, the hero-worship. I find all that embarrassing. I've realised that the extravert aspect of being an actor is quite painful. I'm not naturally gregarious, and if I have to be an exhibit myself then there has to be a good reason for it. For more than ten years now, I'm happiest if the work I'm doing is politically justified. I had an agent who said I had to decide if I was an actor or a campaigner (I had rejected yet another job which I thought presented a disabled person in a negative light). I replied I was a campaigner first and an actor second. I use acting as a means to change the world.

"When I was leaving school in 1969, there were no opportunities for disabled people to become actors. Drama schools, the BBC were simply not interested if you told them you were in a wheelchair, and they made all sorts of pathetic excuses for not even offering you an interview or audition. At that time, the only person who had succeeded in making a career as an entertainer in a wheelchair was Michael Flanders, one half of the comedy singing duo known as Flanders and Swann, and he had already been an established entertainer before he acquired his disability or so I was told. So, I was basically told to get lost.

"However, Michael Flanders who was my role model and mentor, told me that the only way I was going to get into showbiz would be to create my own opportunities, write stuff which only I could perform, create a unique niche in the market. I also thought the only way would be to become a millionaire and buy a film company or TV studio, then I could direct and act in anything I want. So for a while I toyed with become a businessman or going into advertising, become a director of TV commercials and from there into movies, and then give myself the best roles. However, by the time I got to university I rejected capitalism and veered towards radical Left-wing politics, so entering Big Business was no longer an ethical option. By then, I had been involved in disability theatre work-shopping, and it was suggested to me by a former lecturer, Richard Tomlinson, that he and I establish a theatre company of disabled people, hence in 1980 Graeae was formed, which gave me a platform for strutting my stuff."

How important is Graeae to you?

"Graeae is important to me today because after thirty years it has continued to provide training, and opportunities for disabled people to be professionally employed in theatre as performers, writers, directors or in stage management. Personally, as far as my career is concerned, not that important…the last time Graeae offered me a job was in 1996, and that was ten years after the last job I did with Graeae, so although I helped set up Graeae, and I worked with them during the first eighteen months, by the end of 1981 we went our separate ways, and I leapt freelance into the shark-invested waters of the Body Fascist mainstream."

You famously write, direct, act, are an artist… do you see a distinction between the different performance arts… if so what, apart from the obvious demarcations?

"I'm a story-making artist, and writing, directing, acting and painting are all different methods or elements of making stories, each with their own differing levels of autonomy, control and collaboration, so they all have their pros and cons, and they all exercise different aspects of your creativity. Which medium or method for expressing your creativity also depends on how much you want to own the story, ensure it turns out as close to how you imagine it. If I have a story I want to tell, then ideally I need to be in control of as many of the stages and processes possible. So I almost have to be a megalomaniac, the minimum I have to be is the writer, the producer, the director, and possibly the lead actor or an actor in one of the crucial parts…unfortunately unless you're a Mel Gibson or Clint Eastwood or Kevin Costner or Orson Welles, you're unlikely to get the funding for such a privilege…or you are able to work with a tiny budget paid for, out your own pocket…then you can really tell the story as you imagine it to a bigger audience. Whether I paint, write, direct, edit or act, they all satisfy my creative urges in different ways…in the same way my five senses stimulate my brain in different ways…actually, we've left out music….I also enjoy creating soundscapes and music. In fact, one of my regrets is that I'm not an accomplished musician. I have music inside me, impatient to be expressed, and so one day I have to learn to play an instrument to set it free."

Did you follow Doctor Who *before you were cast as Sil?*

"I was ten when *Doctor Who* began in 1963, and sadly, I missed the very first story (because the staff in the children's home thought it would be too frightening.) However, a few weeks later, when the Daleks arrived I was at a friend's house for tea, and he was already hooked, so I got to see the programme and when I did…that was it, I became a fanatic. For the next twelve years *Doctor Who* was my most favourite TV programme in the Universe, nothing could knock it from the Number One spot…*Star Trek?* No way. *Lost in Space?* Forget it. *Man From Uncle?*

"Almost but within a year I grew out of that one. *Monty Python?* Second place. *Thunderbirds?* Never. Once my balls dropped, *Top of the Pops* quickly toppled the heroic puppets. Nope, *Doctor Who* had me in its grip until 1975 when I got to university, then I stopped…mainly because television was no longer the most important thing in my life. However, I still dreamed of one day being in the series. That was an ambition ever since I saw the Daleks in 1963.

"In fact, I would write scripts, story ideas…even wrote a letter to the BBC when Roger Delgado died, suggesting I should play the Master…and that was before I was a professional actor. Also when Peter Davison was leaving, I wrote to Nathan-Turner and suggested I should be the next Doctor, but Colin got the job instead. Now you know the secret of Sil's motivation when he is so venomous towards the Sixth Doctor."

How did you get the part?

"Martin Jarvis and his wife recommended me to Ron Jones, director of 'Varos' when he was still desperately searching for the right actor to play Sil. Apparently, they had seen me perform in an *Arena* TV documentary about Graeae in 1981.

How did you approach such a unique character?

"With extreme care....No, seriously...through his laugh. When I first read the script, I instinctively knew his laugh was the key. Philip Martin the writer, had placed especial emphasis on Sil's laugh as being the defining feature for the character. As an erstwhile Whovian, I knew all the successful monsters, baddies, aliens had one distinctive idiosyncratic gimmick which could be mimicked in the playground, the most obvious example is the Daleks' Nazi histrionic electronic "EXTERMINATE". A friend's pet snake with its flicking tongue gave me a clue as to how to create Sil's laugh. Then, the more I practised the laugh, the more I felt Sil's slimy essence slithering down my tongue and tunnel deep down into my being, until I became possessed by this evil Inter Galactic Megalomaniac Money Grabbing Cringing Cowardly Sadist Bully who is in desperate need of a good loving partner.... Actually, I read someone describe Sil as the Uriah Heep of *Doctor Who*. I liked that, because that memorable Dickensian character was one of the screen models I had in mind when creating Sil."

Did you see a great backstory in Sil? You returned in Colin's next season too... with devastating consequences...

"I can always make up a great backstory in Sil...I have always had an overactive imagination...that's why when I was a kid, adults would never

160

believe anything I told them…even when I knew it was true…so if I said I saw a ghost, and I believed I had, they would say I imagined it…or once when I heard a woman scream from a inside a caravan, and then saw a man as I looked through the window holding a knife…and he saw me…it was one of the scariest moments in my life…I'll never forget the scream…it froze my blood….when I rushed back to the adults in our caravan (it was a seaside holiday caravan site) no one would believe me…they just thought it was my overheated childish imagination…they were so used to me entertaining people with stories…but I never claimed my made-up stories were true.

"So, Sil provided me with plenty of inspiration for creating a history of his life. Returning to play Sil in 'Mindwarp' was a wonderful opportunity, and I did it with relish, partly to get Mary Whitehouse who had apparently written letters of complaints to the BBC about my evil and sadistic portrayal. Unfortunately, the BBC listened to her, so the new script was very much toned down, and Sil was written more as a comic light-weight character. I preferred the darker Sil. I also wanted to give him my best shot because I felt I owed it to his fans. Without their support, the BBC might not have brought him back."

Sil isn't the usual "evil" bad guy, is he? His motives are a lot more shades of grey…

"No, of course, he isn't. I don't believe in "black and white"… "evil" is not as simple as that. Motivations that lead to acts of evil are very complex, and depend as much on circumstances and the environment, and the current morality. When a soldier (or policeman) employed by a government or monarch, kills unarmed civilians, including women and children whether in Iraq, Afghanistan or Israel or in a railway station at home, society rarely accepts that as evil, but if it's an individual (a serial killer or mass murderer) or a militant dissident organisation (labelled "terrorists" by one side, partisans or freedom fighters by the other) who have not been given the State authority or licence to kill, then invariably the media and governments shout "Evil". In the real world of humans "Evil" can be a relative word, especially where rulers and opposing religions are concerned...or maybe I should say what is considered criminal behaviour is relative. It's only in fictional drama and fairy stories, legends and religious myths where good and evil is "black and white". As an actor, I would find it boring and too easy to play a caricature or cliché "evil" bad guy, it is far more interesting to add shades of grey to the character...it makes the character more believable, and consequently more frightening...may be that's why Thatcher's government didn't like Sil, and took *Doctor Who* off the air, they didn't like seeing themselves portrayed on government licensed television."

You're very vocal in your outrage of the Bush administration and the War on Terror... do you see things changing now Obama is in charge?

"How can it change? Change is a word that has lost all meaning. It's just a "Buzz-word". Since 1997 it has become fashionable to preach "Change". Tony Blair was supposed to have been an Agent for Change, but he showed that he was just a closet Thatcherite, and consequently, nothing has changed for the better.

"And when I heard Obama mouthing the same tired slogan as Blair, I thought, "Oh yeah, Obama has come from the same stable as Blair, and will turn out to be yet another puppet of the Right". You don't become President of America unless you've got the support of millionaires, and they will be expecting a return for their investment. Ultimately he is still a servant of the Military-Industrial Capitalist Corporations, and it is not in the interest of the wealthy ruling elite to give up their American New World Order agenda.

"Already, we see Obama has no intention of stopping America's war-mongering. There's too much money to be made. "

What drives you?

"I'm a Natural Born Rebel, who hates injustice, hypocrisy, autocracies and inequality, and I've always had sympathy for the underdog. Anyway, fighting to make the world a much better place is far more interesting than being a greedy, selfish Capitalist pig."

You contacted Russell T Davies with ways of bringing Sil back to you... is he a character you find hard to leave behind?

"It's not that I find Sil hard to leave behind, it's just that he has so much more potential, there is still much more fun to be hard with him, because he seems so complex, and has a capacity to be loved for his very evilness...He is like a Shakespearean character you can never get tired of. Sil is not quite predictable. He is capable of doing good if he thinks it will do him good.... in that sense he perfectly understands the notion of "I'll scratch your back if you scratch mine".... that's the fundamental difference between him and the Daleks, which I think makes him more interesting. "

How did you find your contact with the new series production?

"Negligible. They had no interest in communicating with me. They treated me as if [i]I had never worked in *Doctor Who*."

And now you have a chance to resurrect Sil again in Mission To Magnus... how did that come about?

"A phonecall from my agent, saying Big Finish wanted to know if I would be interested in resurrecting Sil again in 'Mission to Magnus'. Naturally I said "Yes". I had already been offered it back in 1985 after 'Varos', even signed a contract AND got paid because the BBC had to break the contract when the series was scuppered by the villainous Edarg. So, since I had unfinished business, I had to say 'Yes' to a third helping of Sil, even though I am to be heard but not seen."

Can you tell us something about the story, and how Sil has evolved since he last met the Doctor?

"Basically, Sil is helping to organise with the Ice Warriors, Climate Change on the planet of Magnus...a bit like what he is secretly doing on Earth at the moment with Global Warming....so that it is more environmentally friendly to aliens who prefer a touch of frost, and what he hopes to gain by turning Magnus into a frozen planet, is to corner the market in Winter-wear. He is also surrounded by lots of lovely ladies who see men as a menace, and so wipe out boys who reach puberty.

"Actually, doing audio is a disadvantage when the story has Sil being pampered by so many gorgeous women. I miss out on the action, and you don't get to see Sil's tail quivering crazily and suggestively, beating up and down, as he is being caressed.

"In this story, Sil shows he is quite flexible, and capable of changing his colours, depending on which way he sees the wind blowing. Sil is only interested in looking after Number One, so he will readily switch allegiences, if its in his best interests."

164

You say on the Big Finish Website you thought you might have difficulty bringing him to life again, especially on audio... how so?

"It was a long time ago (he says with a quavering ancient voice) twenty years or more. Could I remember what Sil was like? Since then, I had played many different roles...Hamlet, Jesus Christ, Ayatollah Khomeini, Haile Selassie, Mack the Knife and most recently Marquis de Sade...to name but a few.

"Mind you, Sil would have had much in common with Mack the Knife, and de Sade. To remind me of what Sil was like, I had to watch 'Varos' again just before I did the Big Finish job. Also for audio I wasn't going to wear the Sil cozzie and wear the make-up, which I assumed would be vital for me to get back into character. Maybe I should worry that it was actually quite easy for me to revive Sil without all the gubbings, because that suggests I really am Sil....cue gurgle-gurgle...

"Another thing, acting is not only helped by the costume and make-up etc, but also by being on the set or location, and working in physical proximity with the other actors. These all help to make the story or situation real, so you can act with conviction. Even though I've done a couple of radio dramas, I still was unsure if I would be successful in reliving that obnoxious slimy Thatcherite Sluglike Toad. You rely so much more on the strength of your imagination to perform effectively on audio."

How was it working with Colin and Nicola again?

"A dream come true. I love them both to bits. It was like being caught up in a time warp. I swear the TARDIS had transformed into a recording booth."

165

Sil is very specifically a Sixth Doctor adversary… could you see him working with other Doctors?

"Sil doesn't work with *Doctor Who*, he works against him…or rather that damn "DuckTurd" insists on working against Sil, who is, after all, just trying to earn a bob or two. Sil will continue to exploit and rob and try to dominate, and he will fearlessly and fiendishly take on any Doctor the BBC care to throw at him."

Would you resurrect Sil again, for more Big Finishes or perhaps the New Series?

"Sil is always happy to be resurrected. If the "DuckTurd" can be rejuvenated, why not Sil? If Anthony Hopkins as Lecter can be resurrected then why not Sil (Hopkins, by the way, owes me royalty payments for Sil's laugh…. LOL). Sil still feels he has old scores to settle with the Doctor. Actually, I think Sil should have his own series. I mean, lets face it, if that stupid garbage-can of a mutt, K9, can have it's own series, why not Sil?"

Do you still follow the series? What do you think of Doctor Who *nowadays?*

"No because I don't watch telly anymore. But I'll be quick to watch *Doctor Who* for homework purposes if I'm asked to be in the New Series."

Nicola Bryant

Nicola Bryant also spent some time discussing both her Doctors with me...

What made you take the part of Peri?

"I can't imagine turning it down! I was straight out of drama school and this was a wonderful opportunity. Peri was a brave, intelligent, fun girl with a slightly sad and interesting childhood. It was a very exciting role to be offered."

Do you think she ever fulfilled the potential you saw in her?

"In many ways yes and in some ways no. There was one episode that I felt was not at all typical of the character of Peri and sometimes the show resorted to some clichés but I think I was lucky to work with such writers as Robert Holmes, Philip Martin, and Peter Grimwade. I don't want to sit here moaning about what might have been I always find that to be in rather poor taste."

You were part of Who during a time of change, from 45 min episodes to a 12 part series – were you aware that it was a different time for the series?

"Was it difficult to come into an established cast? Well in some ways yes. It was an emotional time for Mark, being his last story but as each story has a new cast and a new director I was in the same boat as everyone else and both Mark and Peter made me feel very welcome and I was very much under the wing of JNT."

Do you think The Twin Dilemma *is unfairly criticised... there are some great performances in it, particularly yourself and Colin.*

"Lots of things are unfairly criticised. I never let that nonsense bother me. It wasn't the strongest story and it certainly was lacking any budget to help it, as it was filmed at the end of the season. What I shall never understand is the venom of criticism that can appear, not necessarily against *Twin Dilemma* but against any episode of the show. I've read of people wishing to kill Steven Moffat and I saw someone talking about wanting to cut off his hands! Well that's just sick. Love the show, enjoy and if it's not your favourite episode so be it, that's fine. *Twin Dilemma* wasn't my favourite episode either."

How important was the relationship with yourself and Colin?

"In the end it was very important. You want to be able to get on with whoever you're working with. I'm lucky that we did and now we're also the best of friends."

Your first full season is full of some of the highest quality Who ever – were you aware of this being an effort by the production team?

"I just keep thinking how lucky I was t have such great stories – like 'Revelation of the Daleks' and 'Vengeance on Varos', not having seen the show for some years I assumed this was the normal standard, only much later did I appreciate how great they were. "

Did you think the series was too violent?

"No I didn't. I think the filming became braver and more dramatic, the style advanced and I think that made some of the scenes more terrifying.

Each violent event was very carefully considered by the team and I have to say compared to what you could view on the other side on ITV at the same timeslot; *The A-Team* where people were being shot left right and centre and there were no consequences to the violence in their show, we were quite tame but vastly more dramatic."

You've worked with three Doctors – did you approach them differently or to Peri was it just "the Doctor"?

"As with any person in real life your approach to a person is often the reflection of their approach to you. As a sensitive teenager Peri treated each Doctor differently. The script and their characters demanded that."

Do you think Peri is relevant to today's Who audience?

"Of course. Why wouldn't she be? A student in search of some adventure. I don't think that would be hard to relate to."

Would you return? (are you returning for any anniversary stuff?)

"Yes and no."

Colin Baker

And of course, we couldn't speak about the Sixth Doctor era without a word from the man himself...

Colin Baker needs no introduction. As an actor he's a British institution, revelling in evil parts in the famous *The Brothers* or out-acting Paul Darrow in *Blakes 7*, and even getting a chance to shoot the then incumbent Doctor as Maxil in 'Arc of Infinity'.

But it is of course as the Doctor he is best known, from his explosive entrance at end of Peter Davison's swansong in 'The Caves of Androzani' through some of the most tumultuous times in the programmes history, to his famous last words in 'The Trial of a Time Lord' Episode 14 ('Carrot juice, carrot juice, carrot juice', in case you didn't know), Colin was a popular and controversial Doctor in equal measures. Cut short by the then Powers That Be, he didn't get a chance to complete his "seven year plan", peeling off the layers of a complex, three dimensional Doctor to reveal a character of great depth, wit and keen intelligence but with an acerbic, touchy side, something which Christopher Eccleston clearly did too.

So it was with great relief and much good fortune that Big Finish decided to release Sixth Doctor audios, and Gary Russell and then Nicholas Briggs saw the potential in the vision Colin had for the misunderstood Doctor.

I was interested in Colin's take on Charley Pollard and the dynamic he has with his companion for these latest adventures. For the uninitiated, Charley had been a companion of the Eighth Doctor, but a little wibbly wobbly timey wimeyness saw her become the Sixth Doctor's new best friend. Of course, she can't tell him they've met two lives on, but he knows something is up. It's an interesting, unique dynamic.

"I think it's a really clever and imaginative plot line. Charley is a very interesting character and her intelligence and resourcefulness make her a great foil for the 6th Doctor – indeed for any Doctor. The fact that there is clearly something she is not revealing of herself intrigues the Doctor and he is prepared to go along with the subterfuge/secret until she either reveals herself and proves untrustworthy. I greatly enjoyed working with India. She is a bright and very talented actress and has the work/fun balance exactly right. Knows when to deliver the goods and yet relaxes in between takes. We had great fun recording my stories with her – and I hope I get to work with her again. I have been very lucky with all my companions."

It's fair to say that Big Finish allowed you the chance to show exactly where you TV persona was going, was that important to you?

"You're right – Big Finish allowed me to bring old Sixie alive and kicking out of the ashes of 1986 and deliver the kind of Doctor I had in mind when I was so 'rudely interrupted'. I have always found characters that take a while to get to know more interesting than one who whole character is there for you from day one. My Doctor was damaged by his regeneration and the viewers were presented by an incarnation that was tricky to warm to straight off. That, I thought, was brave.

"I always use the analogy of Mr Darcy in *Pride and Prejudice*, who is cordially disliked by Elizabeth Bennett until she realizes exactly why he was as he was and what he was really like. Much more interesting. To make the Doctor appear to be a bragging bully in the early stages took the

171

characters and the viewers on a more interesting journey. A journey that Big Finish has allowed me to begin to complete, although I am sure there are more layers of the onion to be revealed yet – and this is where good writing comes in. There have been some absolutely superb scripts coming out of Big Finish and that seems to be continuing, thank goodness."

And of course it allowed him to re-evaluate his relationship with his on-screen companions, Peri and Mel?

"Of course – for the reasons given in the previous answer. My time with Mel was very short and I have done fewer stories with her than anyone else. All my stories with Peri have to credibly fit in between my 'Twin Dilemma' and 'Mindwarp' (in the Doctor's timeline) but it gives us both the chance to explore elements of the relationship that we were unable to experience in the TV series."

Is the character of the Doctor closer now to how you wanted to play the part originally, or have you tweaked it with hindsight.

"Both Gary Russell and then Nick Briggs have been most supportive in my desire to show the elements of the 6th Doctor and his relationship with his companions and indeed any one else in a more developed way than we were able to reach while doing the series on television. I hope that I will be able to continue to develop and surprise and that I will myself be challenged and surprised by the writers."

Was your portrayal an easy criticism to hang on your tenure, when of course there were many other factors which lead to the hiatus and your eventual demise. Were you unhappy with how you were asked to portray the Doctor? Or with your costume, perhaps? What about the criticisms of excess violence etc levelled at the show at this time?

"No I was happy with everything pretty much – but bear in mind I didn't know at the time how short that particular phase of my Doctor-hood was going to be.

"I am on record as having expressed my wish that I hadn't been persuaded that the costume should be as it was. But I guess it was simply, as most Doctors' costumes have been and continue to be – a reflection of the time in which the programme is being made. The eighties was the era of glam rock – and the costume sprang from that garish time. At least I was on the inside looking out!

"I think the violence bit is a complete red herring. If you compare the Doctors I would suggest that the differences in terms of violent content are minimal. I think the public attitude to TV violence changes however.

"I am sure *Dexter* would not have been as successful in those Whitehouse inspired days. And whereas the Doctor is and must be by nature a pacifist and anxious to find the least damage option as a way out – there must be times when violence must encountered head on.

"But having said that my favourite moment ever in any *Doctor Who* was when Christopher Eccleston said 'Every body lives'! in 'The Doctor Dances'."

And now you're getting a chance to get the eighties persona's teeth into some Lost Stories from that era… what do you think of this idea?

"I was very enthusiastic. It seemed such a natural and obvious thing to do."

And did you have much to do with the selection of the stories? Did they need adjusted much?

"I am not sure how much 'selection' went on. I think that every writer who had written a story for me that had never (for various reasons) been filmed was contacted and those that wanted to take the opportunity to have it recorded on audio entered into negotiations. I wouldn't have wanted to have a say because I was completely unaware that most of them existed. I had read the original script for 'The Nightmare Fair' back in 1985 and I had heard of 'Mission to Magnus'. That was it.

"I can only imagine how much work was necessary. Obviously in vision there is no need to tell the viewer as much about the where, the who, the what as they can see it. The knack of writing good audio is telling the listener all that information without being seen to tell them. Some scripts were easier to adapt than others and occasionally there are moments when the characters simply have to describe what they are seeing/doing in a way that perhaps they would not normally. The fact that those moments are so few is a tribute to the collaboration between writers and adapters."

Was much of an adjustment between the Doctor then and the Doctor now?

"Yes that was interesting. I had to 're-wind' back to a less 'evolved' Doctor to a certain extent – depending on where in our relationship the stories were set. Just because they were intended to be recorded back in the 80's we didn't always have to play the scenes as we would have done then. What has emerged in the stories I have done is that some are very much 'of their time' whereas others have been able to be played in a more 'modern' way. It has been a very interesting process. I have no doubt that the listeners to the stories will have a fascinating time re-visiting some Mark One Sixie with glimmers of Mark 2 emerging."

And of course, on Audio, budgets are limitless. It's interesting to wonder what Doctor Who back then would have looked like with as much support as the new series has from the Powers That Be? Do you ever consider this?

"Well of course one can't help imaging how we would have fared had we had the whole heated backing of the BBC back in the eighties with a controller of BBC 1 who has cited Doctor Who as one of her favourite programmes – along with *Strictly Come Dancing* (whose progenitor, *Come Dancing*, was also axed by the then controller Michael Grade).

"It isn't just that the effects and technology have developed exponentially – it is the pride that the BBC has in the show that has made its comeback so spectacular (on the back of excellent scripts and acting of course)."

And I presume you like the new series? I heard you liked 'The Empty Child?

"It is excellent. You're right I loved 'The Empty Child' and 'The Doctor Dances'. It seems that all my favourite scripts were written by Steven Moffat – so that bodes well for the future as he has taken over the helm now."

And of course, we've had Peter (Davison) returning to the role - would you ever do so? The oft mooted Ten Doctor's spectacular for Comic Relief for instance?

"The *Children In Need* rumour was a load of tosh. Nobody has been contacted and there is nothing planned apparently. I think it very unlikely indeed that I will ever be contacted to play the Doctor again – the thirty intervening years have taken their toll and I no longer look like 'Old Sixie'.

"Mercifully however I do look exactly the same on audio. Thank you Big Finish for giving me the chance to offer something more like my vision of the role than I was able to do while playing him on TV."

Colin is a writer of note too, including Doctor Who comic strips. Would he like to write for the series? Or Big Finish?

"Oh I don't think that is likely. I might seize the opportunity to write for my Doctor again, though. Who knows? I love writing and keep meaning to get down to it. But then I get distracted by offers of work!!"

What about an autobiography? I'll help!

"Yes I shall at some point be doing that – thanks for the offer of help but I was there when it all happened so can manage on my own."

So Colin, what's in store in the future? What have you got coming up?

"Lots more Big Finish hopefully – until October 2009 when I get my driving licence back (after a six month ban for speeding) and I can stop turning down work in the theatre."

How like the Doctor, breaking the rules.

The Seventh Doctor Era

Come on Ace! We've got work to do!

'The Trial of a Time Lord' – effectively a full season of *Doctor Who* – was a metaphor for the series itself. After an 18 month hiatus it returned in a blaze of glory – a blaze which eventually grew beyond control as script editor Eric Saward and producer John Nathan-Turner came to loggerheads on the finale of the season.

As a result, Saward moved on, and once again John Nathan-Turner found himself at the helm of a rudderless programme – and one he didn't want to be on anymore. He wanted to move on, feeling he had done all he could on *Who* as the longest serving and most controversial of producers. He'd seen the Tom Baker, Peter Davison and Colin Baker eras come to an end, and wanted a new challenge.

But being a BBC staff producer meant he didn't have a choice. Despite being told he could move on if he sacked incumbent Doctor Colin Baker – who was also his friend – he was forced into continuing on the programme, one which would return to midweek transmission and see it regenerate again.

Gone was the Doctor, the script editor and everything associated with the programme. All JNT had was a companion and an old blue box. He needed scripts – and a script editor – immediately.

He found Andrew Cartmel, whose vision for *Doctor Who* would resonate for the next twenty five years and beyond.

Andrew Cartmel

How did you start with Doctor Who?

"I wrote a bunch of scripts and sent them off to people. I didn't sell any, but I got a load of feedback and useful compliments, and I was invited to the BBC script unit, to encourage people like me, and from there, I managed to make some useful contacts, including Malcolm Kohll[xxxvi], who I'd commission later on *Doctor Who*. He had an agent, and I realised that was the way to get on, so I got myself one and from there I got myself onto *Doctor Who*."

Nowadays the job of script editor is effectively the showrunner isn't it? It's a huge job.

Well the title's different – I know Russell then and Steven now have had a bunch of script editors, but those guys do something different from what I did, the more technical side of things. These days Steven Moffat, as showrunner, does what I did, and I did that, as well as script editing. But the job was really split, because Steven is also the producer, so really the showrunner in my day was split between John Nathan-Turner and me, and perhaps the head of department, but he only came out of his cave on rare occasions."

Where there scripts waiting for you? I know Eric had left quite abruptly. Was 'Time and the Rani' waiting for you?

"Yeah Eric and John had a falling out so he left - without doing anything of course, why would he? John then took it upon himself to look for scripts. Episode one (of 'Time and the Rani') was commissioned, I don't think it was written. I don't remember seeing it on my first day though, so I'm not sure it was physically written."

So what was your approach then? You're sitting there, you're first day, brand new job and you think "Doctor Who"! Fantastic? Daunting?

"Well the most daunting thing was leaving a very secure job working with a computer company in Cambridge, so I had to quit that in order to work for the BBC and for something that was not guaranteed. I don't know if I was daunted that it was *Doctor Who* – I liked that it was science fiction, it gave me scope."

So how about those initial tone meetings? Or did they exist? Did everyone sit down and discuss the future?

"Haha, no, no tone meetings. What it was, was Colin was gone, John was waiting to see about the nod for a new series, and when he got that, he went and looked for a new Doctor, otherwise we'd be filming an empty screen. But it was up to John... I had some input, but it was up to John. As for tone though, and whether I was daunted, my head was into the Alan Moore type of comic book – I'd read a *Swamp Thing*, particularly set in space, and this was where my head was at when coming at science fiction, and what I wanted to do. It wasn't a bad place to be at, to be honest, Alan Moore."

So where you happy with Season 24?

"I was particularly unhappy with 'Time and the Rani', and not because I had no freedom, but it didn't represent my feelings or intentions for *Doctor Who*. But more so, from a personal point of view, everyone knew I was the new script editor on *Doctor Who*, friends, family, colleagues etc, and when this stuff came out and it was just crap, my name was attached to the crap and they blamed me for it. With the wisdom of years, which is something I'd do now, in hindsight, is say 'OK, you can force me to have

179

to put this script out, but I don't want my name on it. You can put my name on things I'd actually script edited, but not this.'

"If I had been script editor on that, the first thing I would have done was sack the writers and do something else entirely. It didn't just damage me, it seriously damaged the show. Here we were coming back with effectively a new show, and of course a brilliant new Doctor, and 'Time and the Rani' was a diabolically bad show and people hated it. I'm sure there are people out there who like it, and think it's a very good story, but they're in the minority, and it was an awful story at best, put particularly to introduce a new Doctor and reintroduce the show."

John was hoping Colin would stay for that story wasn't he? To pass the baton?

"He wanted him to do the regeneration scene, but Colin was very pissed off and quite right too. I'm not sure how accurate I am, but as far as I can surmise, Michael Grade hated the programme and had tried to kill it off.

"He'd put it on pause then brought it back then basically told Colin Baker to get lost, so Colin was so pissed off he wasn't going to come back, so we ended up having to film his old clothes and a Colin Baker style curly wig! And it wasn't particularly effective, but it was all we could do at the time. Again, in hindsight, we could have gone without a regeneration and just started with a new Doctor, like Russell did, but that didn't cross our minds."

I told Andrew about my conversation with Colin, and that it basically confirms his opinion added that, as an actor, Colin couldn't commit to the perception of being the Doctor without the pay-off for another nine months, and that he couldn't, professionally, lose any work.

"And quite right too. Colin Baker is a very good actor, and a very nice man, but I feel the persona of the Doctor that was crafted for him was all wrong. They gave him this callous, bad taste Doctor – his clothes, his cracking jokes, and that awful, awful costume – you could put Sean Connery in that costume and the game's immediately over.

"And the scripts – I felt the 'Trial of a Time Lord' was a terrible, terrible chapter in the history of *Doctor Who* because, on the one hand John wanted to do one big powerful, kick ass story, so he created the trial, but that was awful. He framed everything in this crappy, crappy meta-story, this Master story which folded around the story, and the individual stories weren't all that great, so it didn't work.

"I mean, Eric did some wonderful stories – hampered by some terrible special effects, but that was just where we were – but the scripts had reached a new low, the persona of the Doctor had reached a new low, with some nasty stuff, and I can kind of see where Grade was coming from. I'm not sure if it's true, but I kind of assumed it was 'Vengeance on Varos' which flipped him over the edge as it's quite dark, and has a sadistic element to it, which is ok inasmuch as it being a commentary on video nasties – but there isn't a place for that in *Doctor Who*. It's great science fiction, just not very good *Doctor Who*.'

It's curious that RTD and Steven Moffat have also gone for that linking theme though...

"Yeah but if you think about it Eddie, it's not as rigid as that. It's not linking back to that f**king stupid trial, the arcs they do now, they do by introducing little stories, little plot elements which they thread through – it's not the same as cutting back to this crappy, static, boring bloody scenes about a trial."

181

You did a similar arc with Ace...?

"Well we didn't do it so deliberately; we more or less bolted it on. It was done in a much less considered way."

Season 25 is very well received isn't it? Is this what you wanted to do with Doctor Who?

"Well, after getting passed the debacle of 'Time and the Rani' and getting a new Doctor and a new direction at least begun, we had to get a new companion, because, well, like Colin, Bonnie Langford is a great actress, but the character of Mel is nothing, she's just a screamer.

"I was watching 'Paradise Towers' again recently and the it has a lot of great things in it but as much as I like Bonnie as a person, she just wanders around the corridors, gets captured and screams. If you look at the origins of that character, she's meant to be a scientist, but the character of Mel is a complete dead end. Bonnie Langford comes with a lot of freight too, like the *Just William*[xxxvii] stories, so we needed to replace her, and by 'Dragonfire' we'd brought Sophie Aldred on-board as Ace, so by the start of season twenty-five we had all our elements in place.

"Plus, I'd discovered Ben Aaronovitch, who's one of the best *Doctor Who* writers, with a particular strength in science fiction, so he was just perfect for that job, so I got him to do the Dalek story. There are still problems in that though. I mean, if you look at the Daleks in the Totters Lane sequence you can see them wobbling. I mean, bloody Daleks wobbling!

"And there are other bits and bobs – the time controller is a goddam stupid plasma ball you can buy in Shepherd Bush market. Stupid!"

182

There's a thread in your stories, though, that the Doctor is more than a Time Lord – Kevin Davies for instance, in 'Silver Nemesis', is convinced the Doctor is God...?

"What we were trying to do, Eddie, was build up a sense of majesty to the Doctor and make him larger than he'd been before, so when we were writing for the Doctor, or building him up, when I was, say, discussing it with Marc Platt – who wasn't writing for that season but was part of the team helping to redefine the character – so when I was working with Ben or Marc we'd talking about Gallifrey, Rassilon or Omega, and that was the iconography we were working with. So when I got to speaking with Kevin, he didn't know any of that, so I said "write the Doctor like he's God..." and he's probably taken it literally. That did lead to a problem though because when JNT got wind of that he said "If that gets out they're going to string us up!" but I still say it did the job, and with Kevin putting hints like that in his script it gave us the image of this extremely powerful, shadowy, majestic being rather than the chump, idiot or patsy he'd become in recent years. Obviously though we weren't going to make him God, as being all powerful takes away all the drama."

It's something though that RTD and Moffat have also played with – the lonely God. There's a Messiah thing going on with David Tennant's Doctor.

"I'm intrigued and gratified that Russell followed on with that – it's nice that they ran with that, but I think also dramatically it's a cul-de-sac. Russell also has that problem with Captain Jack in *Torchwood* – the fact that you can't kill him, you just don't want to do that with a character because where's the jeopardy and suspense, what's at stake?"

It becomes the "get out of jail" card?

"Yeah, making Jack invulnerable and the Doctor God kills the drama."

Back to 'Silver Nemesis', the subplots you considered were perhaps too many? Dolores Gray for instance?

"Yep. Dolores Gray[xxxviii] is a brilliant example of this. The thing was that JNT loved to cast stars, right, any star. Whether they were appropriate for the part or the programme or not. He got very excited. He was a big show business type person. He'd come rushing in excitedly and say he'd cast Dolores Gray and to write her a role! And I was like 'who's that?' Now, *now* I know she's a singer, and I'm a big jazz fan, so whilst she's not particularly a jazz singer, I appreciate her now, and I'm a lot more interested in seeing her on screen now, as I was then. That sequence isn't even a subplot. It's just a bit of character colour that adds nothing. It doesn't do any harm, but it's a bit pointless."

With things imposed on you, perhaps, in this way, was that maybe how 'The Happiness Patrol' ended up as it did? Was there talk of the Kandyman being much more different from how he turned out? There's a rumour this episode was going to be filmed "noir" like in black and white?

"Really? No, there was never any consideration of it being filmed in black and white, that wouldn't have been allowed. It *was* meant to be filmed much more Film Noir[xxxix] – some of it is, tilted angles, nocturnal, filmed in the style of *The Third Man*[xl]. That was chiefly because we had an awful lot of problems with the sets being overlit in previous stories and we thought if we set it at night they couldn't over do the lighting. They still did.

"The only thing that was really different was the Kandyman. He was a much more human character, but physical effects came up with that. I thought it was an amazing costume, because it looked just like Bertie Bassett[xli], but I didn't like it because I knew it was a copyright character and it would be trouble later. I know Graeme Curry [the writer –Ed]

184

objected more about it, because it was a big departure from his initial script, particularly in the Kandyman.

"I saw him as being more like the Michelin Man, a big puffy guy made of pink edible stuff like cheap chewing gum, the bubblegum card stuff. Now that would have been virtually impossible to achieve. I think Graeme saw him as a figure made of edible candy, but not differentiated into these separate pieces of liquorice allsorts like Bertie Bassett. More human. It didn't change particularly though."

Was Season twenty-six deliberately darker?

"It was, yes. That's when the Doctor started to wear his darker jacket too, and that helped. It moved him away from that sort of light entertainment look, that sort of ice cream parlour jacket look, and yeah, I don't think the stories are depressingly dark, but they were slightly more adult, touched on deeper themes and they were a little more serious. The Doctor too had reached that sort of stature I'd been shooting for."

'Ghost Light' and 'The Curse of Fenric' are of particularly high quality aren't they?

"I agree entirely, but I'd add 'Survival'. 'Survival' is a magnificent story let down only by the crappy Cheetah People. And the Cheetah People are only crappy because the look cuddly. They look like teddy bears. They never looked dangerous, or feral or menacing. But if you can get your head around that then that's such a marvellous story. I notice we didn't add 'Battlefield' as one of the greats, ha ha. And that was one were the costumes were a big part of it. They were never intended to be knights in shining armour. Ben's notion was that it would be empowered, science fiction armour, like the types you see in movies, in novels and things like

185

Starship Troopers. We wanted something like out of a James Cameron movie, but what we got was this terrible knights' stuff. And there were terrible problems in the way that 'Battlefield' was expressed on screen, to the point now where Ben thinks it's a bad script, but it's not a bad script, it's a terrific script, and it has a great cast, and an enthusiastic director, but it just didn't work. I mean there was a lot wrong with it, but I can't put my finger on what, but it just failed to get across on screen what we wanted to do.

"Every story that season should have been a winner, and I love aspects of them all. As great as 'Curse of Fenric' is, I prefer 'Ghost Light', because, in 'Fenric', we have the Haemovores, and I think they're a mess. A crappy job in terms of costumes. We did get what we wanted with the teenage girls – contact lenses, long fingernails and fangs – proper vampires – and that was kind of the way I wanted to do the Cheetah People, using those kind of elements – so yeah, 'Ghost Light' is the most successful in terms of design – Victorian design is generally very successful because it's something the BBC can do and it understands that. And whilst I think all the scripts of that season are great, 'Ghost Light' comes across best on screen."

I love the Doctor's dialogue in 'Ghost Light'...

"I'm glad you said that, Eddie, he has such wonderful lines. "It's really, really old... perhaps even older!" "The cream of Scotland Yard!" It's packed with witty, twisted, lines. Marc did a fantastic job on that, it's got a myriad of brilliant lines. But you know, even saying that, being really, really pleased with that and saying it's an entirely successful story, there are loads of people out there who just don't get it, who say they can't follow it, and that's something we never had any trouble with in production. So there's that really frustrating aspect of it. I think it had quite a complex backstory though. Some of the end users found it bafflingly complex, though, which I think stops it being an entirely successful story... so unfortunately all the stories had their flaws."

'Survival' is absolutely a template for the new series though isn't it?

"You mean the urban reality thing? Yeah."

Perhaps with Steven going down the more fairytale route with the new series though it's veered away somewhat but episodes like 'Rose' and 'World War Three'...? Is Rose Ace by any other name...?

"Well put, Eddie."

So, that was your three seasons, you're preparing for season twenty-seven and what...? The rug was pulled?

"Yes, the rug *was* pulled, but to say we were preparing for twenty-seven would be an exaggeration. It was pulled whilst still dealing with season twenty-six, so we had no scripts commissioned, just various ideas and themes thought out..."

Would this be the famous Cartmel Masterplan?

"Well, the Cartmel Masterplan! Ha ha. You see, it's only many years later that I heard that term. I always wondered what they meant by it. I always assumed that by the Cartmel Masterplan they meant the plan to put the Doctor back on the rails, make him dark and powerful again, make the show work that way, to return the central mystery to it. That's what the Cartmel Masterplan was, to give us back the majesty to the part. So as far as the Masterplan was, it was done and it worked, if that's what it means.

As far as going further than that I'm not sure that it did."

The Virgin writers guide has a very specific Cartmel Masterplan... Rassilon, Omega and the Other etc...

"Yeah that was developed by Ben, Marc and I because it had to be alluded in 'Remembrance of the Daleks', and Ben expanded on it in the novelisation and Marc did even more in 'Lungbarrow'. But, you see, all the trappings of Gallifrey and all that nonsense I had to attend to with what I was trying to achieve, with the considerable input of Marc and Ben, was give the Doctor his mystery back, but frankly, I'd much rather have had a completely blank slate and complete new start, a dark mystery without any of that nonsense about Rassilon, Omega or the Other.

"Although it *does* correct the Doctor's status as an enigma, it also ties him down and defines him and the ideal situation would be that no one knows where he comes from or why he does things. I always felt that the rot set in when they brought on the Time Lords. As soon as he becomes part of a bunch of other guys then he loses his status in my estimation."

And RTD blows up Gallifrey!

"Yes! Which I thought was quite a good way of wiping the slate clean. He didn't say it didn't happen, like Bobby in *Dallas*[xlii], but it certainly was a good idea to wipe out Gallifrey. The Doctor has to be a one off, a maverick, a loner, a mystery. I also noticed that even though Russell did that, pretty soon we had the Master back on, the Doctor has a wife and a daughter etc... God! Even the passing notion that River Song is the Doctor's wife brings him down, makes him mundane. Terrance Dicks was doing a panel with me once and said that there should never be any snogging in the TARDIS, and he's right! I'm not denying the Doctor a happy life, of course not, but it's not what he's about. It's not that the Doctor should be sexless, but he's got to be on a different level. The way that Terrance put it is that the Doctor would stay clear of relationships with humans because the Doctor has to look at humans as pets, which is pretty profound. It shows why the Doctor can't have relationships with humans in that way – he can be fond of them, of course, but ultimately they're going to die and he's going to outlive them."

It's a frequent criticism to the new series on the forums...

"It's domesticating the Doctor. It's not what he's about. Russell went from the Doctor calling humans stupid apes to him crying over Rose. He comes from a soap opera background, so that's only to be expected. His strength has always been writing characters, and his weakness was writing action and plot, but he got much better at that.

"By the time he got to his third season he was doing a pretty darned good job. I liked David's mischievous character, and him being Scots reminds me of Sylvester. You can see him referencing all the Doctors. And of course, the Doctor is back in a fez!"

What do you think of Matt Smith?

"I think he's been a very good choice. I was a little concerned he was a bit young, but not anymore. He has a fantastic face, like David Bowie in *The Man Who Fell To Earth*. Very alien. I think Karen Gillan was fantastic too!"

Sophie Aldred

If Andrew Cartmel was the master planner behind the McCoy era, other than the Doctor himself, Sophie Aldred's Ace epitomised it. Sassy, feisty, tomboyish and adventurous, she redefined the role of the companion and became a template for Rose Tyler, Martha Jones and Amy Pond. Or is she..?

"I do watch the new series, and I love it. I'd love to think that RTD was thinking about Ace when he created Rose. There are lots of similarities — she comes from a council estate, has a grounding, a single parent, and I'd love to find out whether she is a nod to Ace.

"I think the characters whilst superficially similar, are quite different. Russell uses the assistant as a sort of mouthpiece of the audience, in a way, and that was something that was similar to Ace, and I suppose with all the assistants, but perhaps with Ace, more than before, she was a way for the audience to see the Doctor. To maintain the mystery of the Doctor you have to have a grounded companion.

"That's the similarities, of course, but the differences are that of course Ace had a troubled background, Rose's is less troubled, and her relationship with her mother is far less complex, and because of that, Rose is a much more mature character, her emotions are more settled and mature. For example, her first encounter with a Dalek couldn't have been more different from Ace's.

"So yes there are similarities, and I'd love to think they were deliberate nods, but they're are vast differences which are obviously Russell T Davies's own."

I pointed out the design of the Dalek now was deliberately done to be on an eye to eye level with Billie Piper's Rose, as a direct result of the Dalek in 'Remembrance' calling Ace "small".

"Oh I like that! The amount of detail subtly shoehorned in now fans are in charge is brilliant. That doesn't affect the general audience, but it's a nice little touch thanks to the fans, and, of course, other fans know that too."

Did you feel it was important that Ace was a real character? There are criticisms that perhaps she was more a middle class parody of what working class was like?

"I think the thing is that I was an actress with a part to play, so I do my best to do that and make her as real as possible. It's tricky looking back, because in hindsight we'll always criticise.

"In TV then there was no character like her; she was the first. Nowadays, there are characters like Ace — working class, estate living, single parent etc etc — all over tv, but in mainstream telly then there was nothing. Perhaps maybe *Eastenders* with the Susan Tully character, but at that time and that context it was new. I didn't realise at the time, initially, how new that was, to be honest, because I hadn't watched *Doctor Who* for many years and, really, tv that much. So I wasn't really up on what was going on. I was just doing a job.

"But as I started doing it, and getting noticed, and feedback, and I started to get letters from people I began to think 'gosh, I almost have a responsibility here, a duty of care here, to do this character justice', because so many young women were getting in touch with me saying "this is amazing, I've never seen a character like this before, this is me, I really understand the character of Ace..." so there must have been that it seemed very real to some people. It seemed to catch the mood of the time. You can look back now and think she's a bit dated or stereotypical, but then, well, she was something else. I say, it's all about context."

Do you think the companion reflects the society in which they're in?

"Yes absolutely. I think even when we look back in ten years' time at Rose or Amy Pond they'll seem dated. They mirror the society they're in. I think the function of the companion is to do just that. It's to be the audience. To retain the mystery of the Doctor. Apart from of course when you get the Romana type character, or K9, but to be fair we all know people a bit like Romana in real life. Ace definitely is very much of the late 80s early 90s."

That's happening now. Particularly how Rose and Mickey are compared with Amy and Rory – where getting married is now not a reason to leave the TARDIS whereas Rose couldn't even have a boyfriend!

"That's true! I guess my only beef is that poor old men don't get much of a look in. A kind of pro-feminist emasculation of people propped up again the Doctor himself. Who can compare?"

How important was Sylvester to the portrayal of your character? Are they character dependant?

"They are, they're a great team. It would be great to try Ace with another Doctor, in Big Finish perhaps, but those two are very much a partnership. They go together, don't they? And yet there are, I think, perhaps different attitudes. She'd probably eat Davison for breakfast, be a bit disparaging of Matt Smith, he's a bit geeky, so how would she get on? Tom Baker's Doctor - they'd both explode. She'd get fed up with Colin's and hitting him with a baseball bat! Ha ha. But there was a way that Sylvester's Doctor and Ace grew. And that's a lot to do with Sylvester and how incredibly generous he was at giving Ace an awful lot of the story. I remember one evening watching it live and the BBC announcer actually said "Now it's time for Doctor Who, starring Sophie Aldred and Sylvester McCoy!" Top billing!!! The wrong way round! And that was really quite something.

"But his generosity allowed Ace's character to grow and develop unlike any other companion before. The arc became about Ace and her very strong problems and issues. Also, it allowed Sylvester's Doctor to have more gravitas and depth. If you look at 'Survival' again, it goes to some very dark places with the Doctor."

What did your era do best?

"I think what we did very well was gave a real relationship between the Doctor and companion, which enabled both the characters to develop. Whilst we were watching Ace's character grow and develop, and we were finding out more about her, we also saw the Doctor develop, and saw a story arc there, you know, he started out as quite a clownish, light-hearted character, and ended up being manipulative, dark and not-just-another-Time-Lord sort of thing, thanks to the mystery.

"It also did social comment well too, with writers like Ben and Andrew as script editor, during the Thatcher era, and none of us lot had much good to say about her or what she was doing to the country. I know Andrew had got into trouble with this subversive element in the past, but, you know, it was quite a brave thing to be using as a metaphor, along with anti-racist stuff, Empire comments in Ghost Light etc. It definitely reflected the time."

Did you know much about the lost season twenty-seven?

"Yeah I was gutted to miss out on that. Gutted. I knew talking to Andrew there were vague plans, less than some fans hope, I think, but I certainly know that there was a plan to put Ace on Gallifrey as a trainee Time Lord, which would have been great fun. I don't think Ace would ever have got married – it was different for Amy Pond - unless she could have left him and stayed with the Doctor!"

There's an interesting future with Ace in an old fashioned costume in Windsor Castle... I wondered what that was about?

"Ha, yes! And the lengths that we went to for that portrait. I had a costume fitting, make up, the portrait painted holding the rose. That portrait now hangs in my hall. But I don't think it was intended to be anything other than what it was. Just a funny little scene running down the stairs, but a Madam Pompadour type thing..."

So where is Ace now..? Did she escape Gallifrey? Died in the comics?

"Oh there are so many, take your pick. There are as many versions of Ace as there are writers. All the Big Finish stuff etc too. I'd like to think that Ace was the one who never left, that she'd never gone, and that would be quite intriguing. There was one Big Finish story where Ace does die, she grows old, so there are all sorts of versions. I know too that Russell T Davies mentions her in *The Sarah Jane Adventures* where she's working for some sort of charity, but I thought "Pfft, that's a copout! That's not Ace," but then I thought, "Hang on, perhaps she's working for, you know, Greenpeace or something," She's sort of in the space equivalent of Rainbow Warrior. Direct action in space.

"Someone else suggested that perhaps she's head of *Torchwood* somewhere, that somehow she's involved in *Torchwood*. That's very Ace. Like Martha. That would be great. I'd be very happy for Steven Moffat to write Ace in to any episode! There's been no approaches unfortunately. It would be a shame too if the "real" series (she laughs) isn't marked on telly for the 50th, but it's up to them now!"

Do you think John Nathan-Turner was good or bad for Doctor Who?

"Well the big point is if he hadn't had stayed, *Doctor Who* wouldn't have survived at all, and, of course, I wouldn't have been there, so whether he's good or bad is immaterial because ultimately he's good for it, because he saved it, and gave me a job. There was good and bad things, of course, as a friend of mine's book says.

"I know at the time he was totally slagged off by a portion of fans, that he was a self-publicist, trying to up his own profile. It's true he loved publicity, but that insured it was in the public eye and kept it alive. Some argue that it should have stopped earlier, but I disagree, looking back on my years, they weren't half bad, and we wouldn't have had them if it wasn't for John."

And the stunt casting...?

"Well Sylvester tells a very good story about that, you know, Ken Dodd. Nicholas Parsons (who's very, very good in the 'Curse of Fenric')... was a serious actor before a gameshow host – I heard him in a radio play too and he was excellent... but Ken Dodd, it was a brilliant way to get publicity. That could have worked better if he was directed properly. He says he wasn't directed at all and didn't have a clue what he was doing. Sylvester says Ken was very directable, and wanted to be directed, and yet they just didn't care or presume to think they couldn't. It was less of a casting issue than a directing one, I think."

Parsons is wonderful in 'Fenric', very subtle...

"Absolutely, he still remembers that with a real fondness, and loved it, because it allowed him to show what he could do properly, subtly. It's very well done."

A few words about each of Sophie's stories:

"'Dragonfire' – exciting, for me, my first stab at tv. Everything was just so knew, getting to meet Sylvester and start my lifelong friendship with was just the absolute high point.

'Remembrance of the Daleks' – well for me this is my first story as the assistant and I had to take it on. It was difficult. I was struggling to find the character, but working with the Daleks made it really feel like *Doctor Who*.

The part where I hit the Dalek with a baseball bat has become my defining moment as an actress, it will go with me forever and end up on my tombstone!

'The Happiness Patrol' – now that was good, I felt like I'd found my feet. Sylvester and I knew we were working well together, and enjoyed doing that, I struck up a really good friendship with Lesley Dunlop which was great, and I thought we were doing some really good work.

'Silver Nemesis' – I mean, you know, amazing to be working with Cybermen, who I'd had nightmares about as a child, and to get my own back about killing some off, and brilliantly the casting of the Cybermen were all extraordinarily gorgeous male models, so that can't be argued about it either!

'The Greatest Show In The Galaxy' – Again, another amazingly fun show, a young cast, one big party actually. And meeting up with those guys recently for the release of the DVD has been a ball. We realised it was for some of us the best job we had. Fun in a quarry. Which could sum up the whole of *Doctor Who*.

'Battlefield' – Nick Courtney. Getting to know, and love, and be with Nick Courtney. What a treat. What a blessing.

'Ghost Light' – The complexity of the story which I loved, I loved the setting, I usually loved location stories, but that setting, and the props, and the costumes. The BBC at its finest actually. The calibre of the actors. Sylvia Simms, who still reminisces about it. Frank Windsor. Wow. Fun with evolution.

'Curse of Fenric' – This is my personal favourite. In a selfish, egotistical way, because it's an Ace story. I love how it's written, how the whole idea of Ace and her back story is being explained, and again, lovely cast, that I'm still great friends with. I made lots of friends for life on this programme.

'Survival' – Aptly named! More fun in a quarry! I met Lisa Bowerman[xliii], and I'm still friends with her. A dark, sinister story, juxtaposed by lots of sun, and I was lucky enough to have a Master story. To have Daleks, Cybermen and the Master. How cool is that?

It would be great to revisit that with a bigger, better budget, to redo the

197

Cheetah People. I thought the writing was superb. A female writer with gritty realism was a precursor to the new series."

Andrew wrote the little scene at the end... "There are worlds out there..."

"He wrote that with inklings of what was to come, but Sylvester and I had no idea. We did Ghost Light last. But now of course it has huge resonance. It brings tears to my eyes every time. It's beautifully written, just right for Sylvester, and a perfect end to our tenure."

> There are worlds out there,
> Where the sky is burning
> Where the sea's asleep.
> And rivers dream
> People made of smoke, and cities made of song
> Somewhere there's danger, somewhere injustice
> And somewhere else the tea's getting cold...
> Come on, Ace! We've got work to do...

Notes

ⁱ 'The Man on the Bicycle' was an episode of the series *Suspense*, shown on BBC 1 on 18 March 1963 and starring Carole Ann as Jacky. Future Doctor Who Producer Barry Letts also acted in the series, though not in this particular episode.

ii The first episode is actually called 'The Dead Planet'

iii 'The Girl in the Picture', from series five of *Armchair Theatre*, was shown on 29 November 1964, with Purves in the role of Danny.

iv Purves played the character Terry Buckley in the episode 'Red Hot Winter', screened on 22 January 1964.

v Peter Butterworth (1919-1979) was a British character actor best known for his roles in the *Carry On* range of movies.

vi Michael Gough (1916-2011) was a Tony Award-winning English actor and one-time husband of Anneke Wills, best known in his later years for playing Alfred the Butler in Tim Burton's *Batman* movies.

^{vii} Carmen Silvera (1922-2002) had a long and distinguished TV career (making a later *Doctor Who* appearance in 'Invasion of the Dinosaurs'), but is best remembered today as Madame Edith in the eighties' sitcom *'Allo 'Allo*.

^{viii} *Z Cars* was a popular police series, devised for the BBC by Troy Kennedy-Martin, which ran from 1962 to 1978 and made stars of many of its cast.

^{ix} *Blue Peter* is the longest running children's show in television history. First broadcast in 1958, the show is still running today, presenting a mixture of entertainment, news and activities for British children.

^x *Kick Start* and its spin-off show *Junior Kick Start* showed members of the public taking part in motorcycle trials competitions. It ran from 1979-1988.

^{xi} *The Office* was an extremely successful mockumentary-style sitcom, written by comedians Ricky Gervais and Steven Merchant.

^{xii} David Dodimead (1919-1996) was a British actor. He played Barclay in 'The Tenth Planet'.

^{xiii} Patrick Barr (1908-1985) was a British actor, who played Jack Hobson in 'The Moonbase'

xiv Though it's not clear which publication this quote originally comes from, it appears to have been the basis of the 12 September 1969 edition of the *New Zealand Listener*, Vol

62 No 1561 (p14: Review in 'TV Audience' section, 'Stories in Time' by 'R.M.'), which notes 'William Hartnell - who has just relinquished the role to Patrick Troughton - was very human and warmly appealing… with the change from William Hartnell to Patrick Troughton the very substance of the series lies in the melting pot')

xv William Claude Dukenfield, better known as W.C Fields (1880-1946) was an American comedian and actor, famous for his misanthropic character and bulbous nose.

xvi Speech at the Panopticon convention, 1986

xvii Maurice Chevalier (1888-1972) was a French actor and singer.

xviii The Corona Stage Academy was a drama school set up by Rona Knight in the 1940s. It closed in 1989.

xix *The Young Jacobites* is a 1960 movie, in which Hines played a child, Angus, who travels back in time to help Bonnie Prince Charlie.

xx Shaun Sutton (1919-2004) is best known as Head of Drama at the BBC from 1969 to 1981.

xxi *Alice*, a play by Dennis Potter, was shown on BBC television on 13 October 1965, as part of the *Wednesday Play* drama strand. Concerning the life of the author Charles Dodgson (better known a Lewis Carroll), Deborah Watling played the title role of Alice Liddell.

xxii The 'Radio Times' is a popular tv and radio listings magazine in the UK.

xxiii Bernard Bresslaw (1934-1993) was a British actor, best known for his appearances in the Carry On film series.

xxiv Roger Delgado, the original Master in *Doctor Who*, was killed in a road accident in Turkey in 1973.

xxv 'Carnival of Monsters'

xxvi *Peter Grimes* is actually a section of George Crabbe's poem 'The Borough'. It was later made into an opera by Benjamin Britten.

xxvii HTV was the Welsh licensee for commercial television in the UK until 2008.

xxviii *The Hands of Orlac* (also known as *Mad Love*) is a 1935 Hollywood movie, starring Peter Lorre as a surgeon who transplants a murderer's hands onto the arms of a rival in love.

xxix In Greek myth, Persephone was the daughter of Zeus and Demeter, and queen of the underworld.

xxx *Jason and the Argonauts* (1963) in which Ray Harryhausen had seven living skeletons fight.

xxxi *Soylent Green* was a 1973 science fiction movie depicting a dystopian future, which starred Charlton Heston and Edward G Robinson.

xxxii Traditionally attributed to the poet Homer, *The Odyssey* is an epic Greek poem which recounts the travails of Odysseus as he attempts to return home after the Trojan War.

xxxiii John Webster's *The White Devil* is a revenge tragedy from 1612.

xxxiv British actor on stage and screen. Most famous for is roles in Ealing comedies, and in the St Trinians series.

xxxv *The Golden Voyage of Sinbad* (1973) starred Baker as Prince Koura.

xxxvi Author of 'Delta and the Bannermen', and later a film script writer.

xxxvii *Just William* is a tv series, based on the children's books by Richmal Compton. Langford played the lisping, screaming Violet Elizabeth Bott.

xxxviii Dolores Gray (1924-2002) was an American star of stage and film, and sometime singer and cabaret artiste. She played Mrs Remington in 'Silver Nemesis'.

xxxix *Film Noir* is a cinematic term used by critics of a certain type of melodramatic movie, with a visual style which stresses low key lighting and stark lighting contrasts and which emphasises cynicism and pessimism in its leads.

xl A 1949 film noir thriller directed by Carol Reed, based on a novel by Graham Greene.

xli Bertie Bassett was the mascot of Bassett's Sweets, and did indeed very closely resemble the Kandyman. The BBC promised Bassett's that the character would not appear again.

xlii Infamously, an entire season of the US show *Dallas* – one in which the character of Bobby Ewing was killed - was revealed to have been merely a dream.

xliii Later to play Bernice Summerfield in the Big Finish Benny range.